BE A
MILLIONAIRE

A compendium of Personal Finance for Middle class Indian
With especial reference to northeast

BE A
MILLIONAIRE

YES, YOU SURE CAN!

G.P. Baroowah

PARTRIDGE
A Penguin Company

Cover Design:

Satyajit Baruah
Accenture LTD.
Bangalore, India

Cover photograph:

Dr. Anjan Bhaumik
CAL STATE UNIVERSITY
Los Angeles. USA

Partridge books may be ordered through booksellers or by contacting:

Partridge India
Penguin Books India Pvt.Ltd
11, Community Centre, Panchsheel Park, New Delhi 110017
India
www.partridgepublishing.com
Phone: 000.800.10062.62

CONTENTS

DEDICATION

P.G. Baruah
Editor, Assam Tribune
and to millions of young investors of the country,
Learning to save and invest

G P Baroowah

PROLOGUE

This is a book on empowerment for planning Personal Finance, especially for Indian middle class with a stress on the investors from North East. Nobody can live decently without making provisions for food, shelter and cloth. For human being to provide for above provisions wealth creation is necessary. Even monks need money for sustenance. The great prophet like Swami Vivekananda once said that no proper worship would be possible with empty stomach. To keep feedings one's own self human beings would need provision even when they stop earning. To enable people to meet both the ends it is imperative to save and invest money keeping in view the risk adjusted return. People, now a day, enjoy much longer life than before. To enjoy the life people need to remain healthy. This necessitated the emergence of Personal Finance for security of family members, for continued better health and for better livelihood even during the retired life of human beings. The planning for Personal Finance has become very important in modern time. It provides security for the family and ensures satisfying life.

This book is an attempt to make our young citizens much more investment savvy. It is not an effort for spoon feeding. It is a book to empower young investors to start saving and ultimately aspire to be a Millionaire. This is not just a copy book or hand book of notes that would make investors millionaire automatically. This is a book of empowerment only. The decision for personal Finance must be made by investors themselves. The essays of the book would only empower the mind and inspire to take own decision honestly and truthfully.

The most of the articles of the book was written from 2008 till 2012. Though economic conditions of the country has vastly changed yet the principle of investing has remained unchanged. Readers need to analyse their thoughts rationally always with the passing of time. I have given lot of reference of experts, financial advisors, even of some of the news papers and magazines available in the country. Read those regularly to equip you for the challenging task of investing.

The rise and fall of Share market, beside accident, health and life insurance can not be predicted. To provide for self pension is even more difficult. The patience, robust common sense and capability to take risk would be the most required virtues to be a satisfied investor. This book is meant for inculcating those virtues. It narrates the example of successful persons. The stories need to be read carefully and develop one's own skill. If investors of our country are serious then only this book will inspire them to develop a balanced, healthy and secured mind.

The risk taking capacity of each individual is unique. While making investment this virtue of risk adjusted return for each individual shall have to be calculated depending on the individual capacity. No coaching class will be able to create a common platform for all types of saving and investment. The book has case studies as stories so that young investors understand steps to be taken in a lucid manner. There is no short cut to become a millionaire unless you are a magician, inheritor of wealth, owner of lottery or a black marketer. This book explains that wealth can be created in an honest way. Even a domestic help can become a millionaire, with strong will force and proper guidance.

So, read this book, try to understand the implication and create your own strategies and model and go ahead and make money. For making money you need self restrain & wisdom. No outsider can make money for you. It would be your own perception that would help you to become healthy and wealthy. The articles of this book were published by the Assam Tribune on a regular basis. I must thank the Editor of the paper for requesting me to write the column on each Monday. Eminent Journalist edited the articles before publishing in the news paper. But the chief editor of the book was Dr. Satyaki Saikia. Professor Solomon, Harvard Alumnus, and well known international author wrote the comment on the back cover. The cover page design was done by Satyajit Baruah of Bangalore. The cover photograph was especially clicked by Dr. Anjan Bhaumik of Cal State University, Los Angels. My sincere thanks are due to all of them. I received lot of reactions from my readers too all the time. I am indeed grateful to them. Hope they would be satisfied with the publication of the book.

GPB

CHAPTER ONE

Introduction to Personal Finance

PERSONAL FINANCIAL PLANNING IS
NEEDED FOR A HAPPY LIFE

We all have desires to fulfil and goals to achieve in our life. Unless someone leaves behind a vast estate, we need to earn a livelihood to maintain ourselves and our families. We need money for essential expenses like food, a home, our health, our children's education and marriage; and once the basic needs are met, we need finances to buy a car, to afford family vacations, maybe even build a dream home, and ultimately, plan for a comfortable retirement. These are all attainable goals if we start planning from the beginning of our careers. However, without financial planning, we may reach middle age and start to wonder, "Where has all my money gone?" "Will it be at all possible to reach my goals in life?" Regardless of our stage in life, income, or wealth, a personal financial plan helps clarify and prioritise our goals and set objectives for reaching our targets. Actually, meticulous financial planning is a must for a secure, satisfied and purposeful life.

In Indian culture, four tenets have been specified for a meaningful life on earth for every human being. These are *Dharma, Artha, Kama* and ultimately *Moksha*. These four elements are considered essential for a peaceful and successful life. Very interestingly, among all the virtues *Artha* has been given an important position. Its place is right after the tenet of *Dharma*. What is *Dharma*? Dharma is the expression of divinity in the human body and soul, and *Artha* is one of the basic requirements to keep the body and soul together on earth. Yet, the least importance is given to *Artha* or "money management" by most people of Northeast India. It has been somewhat of a tradition that the importance of money is never discussed in a family get-together, as parents consider it indecent, or at least improper, to discuss money matters in front of their children. This culture has changed of late and people have become more conscious about the importance of money. Yet the full power of wealth has not yet been realised.

In fact, money does not have any strong intrinsic value of its own. It acquires value as it is handled by people. If coins are kept stored in a pitcher or in a box or in a locker for a few years it loses value. During the sixties, people of Assam used to buy 10 eggs for a rupee. Today, that same amount of money wouldn't fetch even one egg. If a person saved that one rupee in a box, today it would be almost valueless. However, if that same one rupee had been saved in a bank earning ten percent interest, its value today would be Rs. 128.00. That sum, even in today's market, could fetch at least 30 eggs! So it is the person who has to assume responsibility to increase the value of their money over time. This becomes even more important when we consider surviving through the current market conditions.

A portion of our earned income must be saved. Why? Because people can earn money only for 35 to 45 years but they may survive up to the age of 80, if not beyond. To keep our body and soul together we need to save and invest money. In my opinion, this is also why we need to make an extra effort to educate our children to realise the importance of money as soon as they are ten years old.

Financial Planning is a process that

1. *Reviews our current financial position*
2. *Sets goals for the future, and*

3. Creates a plan to achieve these goals

The first steps of financial planning need to be started as soon as a career begins. Yet it is never too late to begin. **We should begin with a review of our current financial position and start with a top down approach**. We need to list our assets and liabilities by adhering to the following simple formula:

Total Assets + Total Savings – Total Debt = Our Position
Monthly Income – Monthly Expenses = Our Cash Flow

We need to carefully tabulate where we are spending money. We generally spend on food, fees, gas, electricity, clothing, entertainment, eating out and travel, etc. We need to find every opportunity to reduce our expenses. Eating out less could save you Rs. 1000 per month. Avoiding smoking could save a substantial sum. Planning travel expenses can save some money. Before starting an investment we need to identify our goals. Would we like to buy a new car, buy a house, or take a vacation? We perhaps save for educating our children after meeting our monthly domestic expenses. To be frank, we need to set a target and a time frame to achieve our goals. It is necessary to draw up a financial plan, depending on our risk profile. As soon we get married we need to invest in a good insurance plan. When our first child is born we should take ULIP. As soon as our children go to college we ought to think of our pension plan instead of their education since banks liberally finance post graduate education. A delay in implementation of our financial plan may deny us success in achieving our goals. We also need to remind ourselves that in life circumstances, rules, and market trends are always changing; so we need to review our plan regularly.

We should always try to invest for the long term to reap a greater benefit. We should not put all our eggs in the same basket. Investment in a bank, PPF, debt fund, and equity and mutual funds should be taken as per our individual risk profiles.

As every year draws to a close, along with new resolutions most investors start planning as to how to go about investing in the New Year. It must be kept in mind that the equity market generally does not provide excellent returns in the short term. 2009 was different and an unusually good year. (As of 28th December, 2009, an investment of Rs. 1 lakh on 1st January, 2009, gave a return of Rs. 1,78,597 on BSE Sensex; Rs. 1,29,953 on Gold; Rs. 160,991 on silver; Rs. 1,08,243 in a fixed deposit bank account; Rs. 1,22,027 in debt oriented hybrid fund, and Rs. 1,86,090 on an equity mutual fund.) The highest return came from equity, followed by silver and gold, and the lowest was in bank fixed deposit.

According to our calculations year to year, returns during each New Year may not be as alluring as it was during 2009. Inflation is getting higher every day. Though America and Europe are out of the severe recession, unemployment figures have actually not gone down. The failure to pay the sovereign debt in Greece, Spain and Italy may create havoc in the Indian stock market. So, if someone has money they should hold on to it and invest when the market goes down further after a few months. But investors should not worry. In the last ten years (from the year 2000 to January 1, 2010) the best return came from equity (despite big crash of 2008), followed by gold, silver, real estate, debt-oriented balanced fund and, lastly, bank Fixed Deposit accounts.

The greatest virtue for the investors in 2010 would be Caution, Patience and Boldness. If you are weak-hearted, do not invest! 2010 will be a landmark year as it will provide the base and create a foundation for successful earnings in 2012-2015. Investors should fix their vision judiciously, keep their earning capacity in mind, and wait for the best opportunities to invest. And trust me opportunity will knock on the market door in 2010.

As a thumb rule investments should be done in the formula of 100—Age = Equity. The balance amount should be saved in a debt instrument. The corporate bond fund of Templeton has started providing a return of 12% now. You can invest in this fund for thirty months and get a tax free return. After reaching the age of 75, no more investments should be made in equity. At that time we need to draw up our will and keep all the money in a bank. Married couples should always have a joint bank account as a measure of security. We will be happier, more satisfied, and more secure the sooner we make a financial plan for our life.

A PERSONAL FINANCIAL PLAN SHOULD BE THE GOAL

Investment without a specific purpose would not lead to a successful and happy life. It would be a meaningless exercise to invest without specific goal in mind. No wealth can be successfully created without goal orientation. To be a successful money manger you need to divide your investments into separate goal-oriented portfolios. Many people have written to us asking for advice regarding investments. Whenever I receive a request for investment advice from my readers, I ask them for three things: their age, their total income, and the purpose of their investment.

"Why do you want to invest?" I ask them.

"Obviously, to make money," most replied.

"What for?"

"To spend in the luxuries of life," some of them replied.

This is a very short sighted objective. It is true that everybody needs money for various requirements in life. We need money for daily living expenses, for medical needs, for travelling, for dining out and other entertainment, for our own marriage, to raise and educate our children, to fund their higher education, to take care of our aging parents, to build our own house, for the wedding of our children, and hopefully, for a smooth and worry-free life after retirement. To achieve each of these goals, people need to start saving money in due course of time. Planning your investments is a serious business and should be done very carefully.

Now, let us analyse the case of a 25 year-old student who completed his studies after post graduation and got a job in a company with a good salary. If he has no liabilities at home, he is fortunate and he can plan his investments and savings from the very first month of his earning. What does he need to do?

Firstly, he would be required to open a bank account to receive his salary. He should plan his finances in a sheet of paper after discussing with his parents, if they are knowledgeable. If not, then he should go to an investment advisor and ask him for help with the plan. An initial sound personal financial plan will help him ensure a smooth future. Maybe, his financial advisor will come up with a plan like this:

1. Open a PPF account and initially deposit Rs. 500/—every month. You can increase the amount after a year when you get your confirmation and increment.
2. You need to open a recurring deposit account for five years to finance your marriage or your honeymoon trip.
3. You need to take a Term Insurance cover for thirty years. The premium will be minimal. However, insurance at this stage is not most essential and you can defer it till you get married. Since medical coverage for you and your parents will be taken care of by the company, you don't need a separate Health

Insurance coverage immediately. In fact, if you always get coverage from work, you can wait till you are in your 50s. You should buy a health insurance policy later in life, but before retirement because once you retire it may be difficult to get a health insurance policy with good coverage.

4. As soon as you are 30 you should subscribe to a pension policy, either through an insurance company like LIC, through a Mutual fund, or through the NPS scheme.

5. Since you deferred the life insurance policy for a while, you can invest at least 20% of your salary in a mutual fund for a period of five years or more. This will give you an exposure to the equity market. Later in life when you start earning more money, you can buy shares of large efficient companies in sectors like banking, IT, and FMCG.

6. You should create an emergency fun to take care of your sudden needs. The emergency fund must be maintained throughout your life.

7. In case you wish to buy a car later in life or build a house, you could utilize the money in the mutual fund for initial payment and take a loan from a nationalized bank for the rest.

8. After marriage your responsibilities will increase and the safety and security of your family should become your first priority and you will have to plan for your children's education. Then you should purchase a good life insurance policy and start a SIP that will eventually fund the education of your children.

If our young man does decide to follow the recommendations above, not only will his future be secure, he will also extend a safety net to his entire family. Investing hurriedly without a plan and without goals will make it a fruitless exercise.

All investors must plan their financial goals if they want to ensure a peaceful and secure future. Hari and Madhu were two friends who studied together, worked together, and retired together. But Hari did not have a pleasant retirement because he did not plan for it in time. He used to tell his friends that his philosophy was to earn money, spend it in the luxuries of life and be happy. Madhu, on the other hand, planned his finances from the very beginning and transitioned easily into a comfortable retirement. Hari started investing late and without goals. Even after retiring, he invested most of the money from his retirement corpus in equity. In 2008, when the market went down, he lost most of his money and did not get any dividend for years. He suffered a lot. All investors should remember that equity is good for wealth creation in the long term. For short term needs, investments should be made in fixed income instruments like a bank FD, debt fund, or in secured debentures of well-known companies.

After retirement you will need money for day-to-day expenses. It will be foolish to invest in the equity market and expect to get a regular income from your investment. The share market remains volatile all the time and you will be in trouble if you invest money in equity to get a regular monthly income. A bank FD or a debt fund will yield a regular income without tension.

What's a good solution to this challenge of managing daily expenses? Some sophisticated analytical tool that will give us amazing insight? No. Actually, it's something that someone in your family probably already practices, or at least used to in the decades gone by. The solution is in bags or in envelopes. My sister, after the death of her husband, introduced the envelope system for day-to-day expenses. Every month she draws money out of the bank and divides it up into categories like: vegetables, milk, dhobi, etc. and puts each amount in a labelled envelope. This allows her to constantly monitor how much money is being spent for which need and adjust accordingly. It also allows her to identify where she might be overspending and where she might have a little cushion to absorb some extra unexpected expenditure. She even has a little "reward" envelope for a treat if she has managed her monthly finances well!

"Curiously, as a principle of budgeting, this is known to most of us but very few of us apply it to have a separate set of investments marked out for each. The monthly income could be in an MIP fund or a post office monthly income scheme. The emergency funds should probably be in a fixed income fund. The long-term money should be in equity funds and so on.

"This enables clear thinking about each goal and the investments that will best meet that goal. For example, if an old couple won't need a certain amount for a decade, then it should be in an equity fund. Long-term investments should be in equity, regardless of the investor's age. In fact, the worst thing that can happen to retirees is to run out of savings and the long-term growth of equity is needed to fight the corrosive, compounding effects of long-term inflation," said Dhirendra Kumar, financial advisor of repute.

WHAT IS THE NEED TO INVEST?

People, of course, need to invest regularly. Some may ask: Why we should save and invest? We need to invest for our future. We earn money during our working life only. If we spend all the money during our service life, what do we do after retirement? "We will get a pension," some one may reply. But every body does not get pension. Even when you do, the rate of pension is about 50% of the basic salary. This amount may not be enough to buy you the basic requirements of life as you age. Inflation may affect your earnings. You need a second source to enable you to relax and enjoy your life after retirement. You may also love to contribute and give back to society which fostered you for so long! You also may not like to depend on your children.

Warren Buffet is a man of frugal habits. He lives in an old house worth only thirty thousand dollars. He has a car, without a driver. He drives himself. He earns 5000% per annum for his clients and shareholders. He has donated 30 billion dollars to charity to be managed by The Bill and Melinda Gates Foundation. A portion of this money, perhaps, flows to North East India to help eradicate AIDS! He is one of the most respected investors in the world and according to Forbes he was the richest human in 2007. Every year, he is usually among the top 3. All of us cannot become Warren Buffet, but we can learn a lot about wealth creation from him. Now the question is how do we invest?

We need to invest where our returns are optimal. Not for today, but for tomorrow. If we save money in a pitcher or in an urn, as our forefather did, we loose the value of money. If we keep money only in a bank, the returns are minimal and subject to taxes and inflation.

So we need to look for avenues where returns are stable, higher, and free from risk and tax. PPF fits the bill, as there is no income tax and the tax rebate is also available. Similar is the case of GPF and EPF. All employees should maximize their contribution to their Provident Fund, i.e. 20% of the salary. But risk free saving does not provide the highest returns. So we need to look at the share market and mutual funds to make real money. I, however, do not recommend jumping headlong into the share market. The best way to learn the nuances of shares is to go through the route of mutual funds. There are various mutual fund companies which launch funds at regular intervals. We can buy units from them directly or through their agents. If you buy directly, no entry fee will be charged. Otherwise a 2.25% entry fee is charged! The next pertinent question is: While investing, what should we consider?

According to the legendary Warren Buffet, the following things should be kept in mind before investing. (1) Don't invest in any product you do not understand. Study and invest. (2) Focus on the long term. Short-term investments do not provide long-term benefit. (3) Buy shares when the market is low. (4) Sell when the market is high. (5) Avoid short-term day trading. (6) Select shares with future potential and not today's hero. Buffet's recommendations are simple and full of wisdom, but many critics have called them naïve! We, however, accept his views as fantastic. Buffet doesn't just preach but sets an example by his deeds.

Since we are not recommending an initial participation in the share market and advising you to take the route of mutual funds, the investor should buy funds from recognized five—and four-star fund houses only. Persons with internet access can consult the website valueresearchonline.com and others should read an investment magazine like *Money*. Younger people should first invest in a Diversified Fund and senior citizens should invest in a Balanced and Income Fund. How much should one invest? There is no rule as such. After meeting the household expenses, you should aim at saving 20%. If that is not possible, whatever is possible should be set aside and saved. How much money should you invest in a mutual fund? A mutual fund can be a risky instrument, so investors can use the formula: **100 – Age = % of equity.** This means that an investor aged 25 years can invest 100 – 25 = 75% in equity, whereas a person of age 65 can only invest 100 – 65 = 35% in equity. After 75 years there should be no investment in equity unless s/he is a high net-worth person. A word of caution: *Invest in equity only if you can spare money for the long term.* Consult a certified financial advisor before investing, and always enter the market through a secure place like a bank, a well-known broker, or directly at company offices.

CAN I REALLY BE A RICH PERSON?

Do you want to become rich? Who does not want to be a wealthy person? Can a person be a millionaire without taking the wrong path? Can a poorer person really become a wealthy person? These are some of the questions which we hear everyday from people around us. Yes, you can become rich without using any dubious methods. The things you do need are will power, patience, and determination to remain in the correct path. You do not need lots of money to start with, but you will need a systematic lifestyle to save money first. The attitude to save is the first step. The second step is to protect the money you have earned. Thirdly, you will need to deploy the money in the correct place. You can save as little as Rs. 650 per month and become a millionaire in 25 years! Yes, time is the essence. I don't have a magic wand to make a person a millionaire overnight. A person needs to work hard and earn from his savings. To be rich, an investor needs four qualities:

1. Frugal habits
2. Disciplined lifestyle
3. Target to achieve
4. Patience to wait for a long time

How to save money? Money can be saved in various ways. It is not necessary that a person has to save and invest only in the share market to get rich. The habit of saving should be inculcated from the age of seven. Do you know that Nationalized Banks allow a child of seven to open an account? You can also buy your child a piggy bank for the seventh birthday. They can be taught to save whatever they get, as presents, during Bihu, Puja and on birthdays from their relatives. The gift of a piggy bank would be the first step to develop the habit of saving in the child. In the USA, many parents ask their children to collect "quarters" (25 cent coins) from each state of the Union. Later, this often becomes a hobby for a budding numismatist.

Young girls and boys can start saving seriously as soon as they start earning. On getting a stable job, they should immediately start a Public Provident Fund account. Next, start a ULIP, insurance, and a regular bank account. The PPF account can be opened in a post-office or in one of the nationalized banks. You can save a minimum amount of Rs. 500 only and a maximum amount of Rs. 1,00,000 per year. You do not have to pay any tax when you withdraw the amount and you get a tax rebate on the amount you save every year! The account has to be maintained for a period of 15 years. After seven years you can withdraw a portion of your savings in case of an emergency. I know of a person (Mr. M.C. Deka of Ugratara) who quit smoking, and his wife collected the surplus amount from his former habit and saved it in a PPF account. After twenty years, she checked her account and found she had saved Rs. 20 lakhs!

Pushpa, a semi-literate housemaid, came from a village to work in the house of a friend. She was paid a sum of Rs. 550 per month. My friend started a savings account in the post-office where she saved Rs. 500 per month, keeping only Rs. 50 for her pocket expenses. Within two years she collected around Rs. 13,000. Pushpa was advised to invest Rs. 10,000 in an SBI Magnum Tax Saving Account in 2002. She did. By December 2007, the amount had become Rs. 1,50,000.00! It was not just a dream but reality. If Pushpa can become a "lakhpati," working as a domestic help, why can our young boys and girls working as nurses, parlour assistants, telephone operators, vegetable vendors, peons, and daily wage earners not become self-made millionaires?

What you need is the will to save and the patience to wait and realize your dream. I also know of a friend (a retired IAS officer) who invested 1 lakh in the same fund in 2002, after his retirement, and got back 15 lakhs in January 2008. Fortunately, he withdrew his money before 21st January. That amount would have eroded by at least 25% when the share market crashed! One thing that must be kept in mind is that there will be ups and downs with mutual funds and the share market. But if you invest for the long-term you will emerge as the winner. Please keep in mind that Warren Buffet became the richest man in the world only by investing in shares and funds for a long time. The first step to become a rich person is to earn money and the second step is to develop the habit of saving. The third step is to invest and protect the money you have saved. You can start your journey with a PPF and slowly graduate to Mutual Funds, then to shares.

A MAID CAN BE A MILLIONAIRE IF SHE IS EARNEST

Nobody can live under the sun without making provisions for food, shelter and clothing. For all of the above provisions, money is necessary. Even monks need money for sustenance. The great prophet Swami Vivekananda is known to have said that proper worship is not possible in an empty stomach. We need money to feed our self even when we stop earning. To enable people to make both ends meet, it is imperative to invest money keeping in view its risk adjusted return. People, nowadays, have a longer lifespan. This necessitated the emergence of personal financial plans in wealth creation. This book is an attempt to make our young citizens more investment savvy. It is not a book that will spoon feed. It is an effort to empower young investors to start saving and ultimately become millionaires. This is not a guide or a magic book of notes that will automatically transform investors into millionaires. No, it will not. This is a book of empowerment.

Savings and investments are not an easy task. Patience, robust common sense, and the capability to take risk would be the most essential virtues to be a successful millionaire. This book is meant to inculcate those virtues. It narrates examples of successful people, both famous and ordinary, but all having the virtues I mention above. The stories should be carefully and used to develop your own skill. If you are serious, this book might inspire you to develop a financially balanced and disciplined mind.

The risk-taking capacity of each individual is unique. While making investments, this virtue of risk adjusted return for each person shall have to be calculated depending on the individual capacity. No coaching class will be able to create a common platform for all types of savings and investments. This book could act as a compendium for empowerment in personal finance. It has case studies in the form of stories so that young investors can lucidly understand the steps to be taken. There is no short cut to become a millionaire unless you are a magician, an inheritor of wealth, the owner of a winning lottery ticket, or a black marketer. This book proves wealth can be created in an honest way. Even a domestic help can become a millionaire, with strong will force and proper guidance.

So read this blog, try to understand the implications, create your own strategies, then go ahead and make money. To make money you need self restraint and wisdom. No outsider can make money for you. It will be your own perception and determination that will make you wealthy.

A DISCIPLINED SAVING HABIT BENEFITS THE INVESTOR

A disciplined investment habit is the mantra for a higher return on capital. After all, everyone saves and invests to earn more and more. If earning the maximum would not have been the motive, all investors would have deployed their funds in small-savings schemes or in the bank. But slowly, people have started embracing risk to earn more money. Shares and mutual funds are comparatively risky but ultimately, this asset class provides better return in the long run. In the short term, shares and mutual funds remain very volatile. No one should invest money in mutual funds and shares unless they have the capacity to withstand some loss for short durations. Is there no way to override the volatility and earn better returns? This really is the proverbial million-dollar question.

There are ways and means to override market volatility. During the month of January 2008 the market was zooming up. Suddenly on 21st

January the market started coming down and within 30 days it had crashed. By mid-April the Sensex fell from 20,000 points to 15000 points. Again, from the last week of April to the first week of May the market recovered and the Sensex again soared to 17,600 points. It went down again during May and June. Well known investment pundits opined that the market would slowly recover only from the middle of July. To override this kind of volatility, investors should plan to invest in mutual funds through a method known as SIP. What is SIP? SIP is an acronym for Systematic Investment Plan. You can invest in any mutual fund in a lump sum amount. You can also invest in equal instalments every week or every month. Say, you want to invest a sum of Rs. 50,000. You can invest it in one go. You can also invest in ten equal instalments every month for ten months. This method of paying by instalments or in a recurring plan is known as SIP.

Who determines the number of instalments in "SIP"? The Investor is the Boss for any investment decision. So it is you who will determine the number of instalments to be paid in SIP. Is there any minimum or maximum numbers of instalments already determined by the fund houses? Yes, according to present practice, the minimum instalments need to be six. But there is no pre—determined maximum number of instalments. It depends only on the investor. You can keep paying instalments regularly for three years or even more! When you buy units of any mutual fund, from a company or from an agent, you have to fill out a SIP form and hand over post-dated cheques. These cheques will be debited from your account every week or every month as you desire. If you prefer ten monthly instalments you will have to hand over ten cheques. If you want to pay in weekly instalments then you need to hand over forty cheques. Is there any other way or system to pay the instalments? Yes, there are. You can transfer a lump sum amount to a liquid fund of the same fund house and give them instructions to transfer the amount every week or every month to the desired diversified or ELSS or Balanced fund. The money in the liquid fund will earn around 8% interest. The money kept in that account will be systematically transferred to buy equity funds as per your instructions. This system is known as STP. I prefer STP to SIP because it is cost-effective. Remember, each cheque issued costs money. There is also a third alternative. You can give a mandate to your bank to transfer money to the mutual fund in desired instalments. Why are SIP and STP beneficial? They are beneficial because in a volatile situation when the NAV (Net Asset Value) of your fund goes down, you can buy more units with the same amount of money. Ultimately, the cost of acquiring units become low so you are greatly benefited when the market goes up in the long run. I hope the matter is clearer now. Go ahead and buy through a "Systematic Investment Plan" or through a "Systematic Transfer Plan."

THE MILLIONAIRE: CHANGING FACE OF THE MIDDLE CLASS

During my four-month stay in the USA, I did some research to find out how most people became millionaires there. Was it mainly through business and investment? Or by following regular habits of saving and investment? To my utter surprise I found that most millionaires in America are new and they are self-made. Meaning, they did not become wealthy from some influential family-business connection, by inheriting land or assets of some community, or from shares of industrial investment, but from working as a service-person and through a regular and disciplined habit of saving and investment. Approximately 33% of millionaires today come from the middle class who never inherited any fortune from their parents. Even Bill Gates' and Warren Buffet's wealth were created during their lifetime and not from inheritance. This is very good news for the aspiring middle class of India.

It is a fact that the United States booms when it comes to creating millionaires. America has the highest number of millionaires in the world since the last few years. The nation counted 8.9 million millionaire households in 2005—that's more American millionaires than ever before, according to British market researcher TNS Financial Services. It was the third consecutive year that the number of U.S. millionaire households rose, and the total number of millionaires has jumped 62 percent since 2002. The study defined a millionaire as anyone who has a net worth of $1 million or more, excluding a primary residence. Even during the period of recession, though the number of millionaires has reduced by 10%, America still boasts a higher number of millionaires than anywhere in the world. I was pleasantly surprised to find that a large number of these millionaires are not only self-made, but professionals: scientists, professors, consultants, lawyers, doctors, business executives, movie actors, and sports players.

What are the most important qualities that made them millionaires? We asked a few working persons who are millionaires in San Jose. They wanted to remain anonymous but confided in us that the two most important characteristics would be (a) the capacity to dream big, and (b) to cultivate enormous patience. There are a few other qualities necessary for building up a fortune, they added. These are frugality, avoiding impulsive decision making, courage, optimism, and self-discipline. In modern times, most millionaires cannot be recognized by their appearance as they remain frugal in habits. Even billionaires like Warren Buffet and Narayana Murthy live in modest homes and drive regular automobiles.

In our quest, some very interesting data revealed that the average millionaire household in the U.S. had a net worth of roughly $2.2 million, and about half of the heads of these households are 58 years or older. Forty-five percent of millionaires are retired persons. The highest number of millionaires in the U.S. resides in California. It's no surprise that Los Angeles County topped the list with 262,800 households qualifying for the millionaire status. While the label "millionaire" may conjure images of business moguls like Bill Gates and Warren Buffet, the TNS study found that just 19 percent of U.S. millionaires made their wealth through all or part of a private business or professional practice. Apparently, the lion's share of the country's millionaires made their money the old-fashioned way, working, saving and investing. This is what inspired me to share this information with the readers because you might also be sincerely trying to become a millionaire, and there is no reason why you cannot. How much time did a regular middle-class person take to get there? About thirty years of regular saving and investing.

What was their main reason for accumulating wealth? TNS reported that the most common goal mentioned by the millionaires in the survey was to "assure a comfortable standard of living during retirement." Lesser financial goals included leaving a big inheritance to children and charitable giving. One of the millionaire technocrats said that to become a millionaire, besides his own qualities described above, it is necessary to have a mentor. Many people have become millionaires because they had good guidance from their mentor. An outstanding example is the driver of Narayana Murthy who also became a millionaire due to his mentor's help.

The U.S. has 8.9 million millionaires whereas Russia has 87,000 and China has 300,000. In my research, I found that one of the highest concentrations of millionaires is in Silicon Valley. When I visited Santa Clara county of Silicon Valley, I was amazed to find that one out of twelve residents was a millionaire. It is a well known fact that Santa Clara is a county of predominantly service-industry professionals who work as consultants, teachers, office executives, bankers, or IT and communications specialists. How much do these professional make? Most of them started with an average annual salary of $36,000, which had climbed to $150,000 in five years, and later rose to $260,000 or more per year. They regularly paid income tax (both state and federal) to the IRS in the highest bracket amounting to 38-40% of their income.

Before World War I most millionaires were landowners. Before and after World War II, most of them were from the business community. In the last sixty years, the profile of millionaires has changed to the traditionally middle-class section of society. By the end of twentieth century, one-third of all millionaires came from the middle class. This definition started including scientists, teachers, IT and communication engineers, business executives, lawyers, doctors, and architects. I would, therefore, like to conclude that the middle-class people of Assam can also become millionaires in terms of monetary value if they save and invest well for about thirty years. Our aim, however, should not only be to become a millionaire but to make a fortune while remaining in the path of truth by dint of our education and beautiful minds. For whom or what do we need money? Initially for our livelihood, then to live comfortably during our days of retirement, and thereafter for the charity of the society that fostered us.

INVESTOR LITERACY IS A MUST BEFORE STARTING ANY INVESTMENT

All investors are not always literate. Even a postgraduate in science, technology, or the arts may not be well versed in savings and investment. Before starting any investment everyone must take some time to learn where *not* to invest and where you should invest. Investing is a personal requirement depending on our goals in life. Besides investing in a debt instrument, it becomes imperative to invest some money in equity to beat the inflationary pressure. Before jumping into the share market, all investors should learn to invest in equity through mutual funds. Investment in equity is a long-term requirement. No investment in equity should be done in the short term. It is my sincere advice to study and wade into the market instead of diving in blind. If the market is falling, let the fall stabilise at a lower value of SENSEX and NIFTY. Then you should start through a Systematic Investment Route.

We all tend to look at the returns of a mutual fund before making a decision to invest our hard-earned money in it. The returns actually denote the appreciation/depreciation of the NAV of the fund. Unfortunately, the NAV (Net Asset Value) of a fund is often grossly misunderstood. Let me attempt to clear the myths surrounding NAV.

Nowadays, more and more people have started investing in mutual funds. This is a good habit. However, many investors make a mistake by choosing a product with a low NAV, thinking that the lower the NAV the greater will be the return. This is a mistaken assumption. The NAV of a mutual fund is grossly misunderstood by investors as well as many mutual-fund distributors. A low NAV does not indicate that the fund is cheap, nor does it impact the returns in any way. Please remember this when selecting a fund for investment. Rather, focus on the overall quality of fund, which will greatly impact your returns. Always choose a fund house with a long history of dividend and growth. Whenever a new fund is launched it does not have a past record or a history of performance, hence it is always better to rely on old faithful funds that have done reasonably well over the years. Many investors subscribe to new funds thinking that a low NAV will make it a highly prized unit. This is incorrect. Please know that even a high NAV might give you a better rate of return most of the time. What is more important is to choose a fund that has a record of consistent returns month after month and year after year.

The NAV or Net Asset Value is the aggregate of the market price of all the shares contained in the portfolio inclusive of cash after deducting the liabilities, divided by the sum of units issued. It can also be called as the book value of the unit of the fund.

NAV = (sum of shares in the portfolio + cash – liabilities) ÷ total units issued

Many people tend to think that a fund with a low NAV is much cheaper than a fund with a higher NAV, and they might prefer a fund that has an NAV of Rs. 50 over a similar fund with an NAV of Rs. 80. This misconception stems from the fact that most people tend to equate NAV with the market price of a share. As a result, there have been instances when people have redeemed their investments in well-performing funds to invest in NFOs (New Fund Offers). Even many mutual fund salesmen tend to mislead people by telling them that funds with low NAVs are cheaper than those with high NAVs, thus enticing them to invest in the funds that they are selling.

There is a big difference between the NAV of a mutual fund and market price of a share. In the case of shares of any company, its market price is decided by the stock exchange. The market price depends on many details like the company's fundamentals, view of the company's future performance and the supply-demand situation. Due to this, the market price of a share usually differs from its book value. But in case of a mutual fund, the concept of market value is absent. When you purchase mutual-fund units, the NAV is simply the book value. This simply reflects the correct price of the assets that you are buying. This price could be Rs. 50 or Rs. 500, but the concept of a higher or lower price does not exist.

While it is commonly believed that funds with lower NAVs will yield better returns, it is not true. Suppose there are 2 funds with NAVs of Rs. 50 and Rs. 100, respectively. You invest Rs. 1000 in both of them. So you get 20 and 10 units respectively. Let's assume that both funds give a return of 50% after one year. So the new NAVs of these funds become Rs. 75 and Rs. 150, respectively. Now, the value of your investment in the first fund becomes Rs. 1500 and that in the second fund also becomes Rs. 1500. Thus, the return in both cases is the same, irrespective of the NAV of the fund. Instead, it is the quality of the fund that will greatly impact your returns.

The NAV of a mutual fund is often grossly misunderstood by the investors and less often by the mutual-fund consultants. A low NAV does not indicate that the fund is cheap, nor does it impact the returns in any way. Always remember this when selecting a fund for investment. Rather than looking for a low NAV, focus on the overall quality of the fund and you will be amply rewarded.

Mutual funds are a good way of developing safe and healthy investment habits. Funds should be bought in terms of their star rating and not in the recommendation of brokers. Always depend on the recommendation of your advisors, but the best strategy is to study and decide what is good for you. Always buy a diversified mutual fund instead of thematic funds. Sometimes, thematic funds promise and deliver high returns. The power sector once gave very high returns but the risk is that if the market turns sour, that sector might suddenly crash. The wise decision is to rely on the value analysis of the rating agencies. The most neutral and dependable agencies are valueresearch. com and moneycontrol.com. Before investing, please study their ratings and take a conscious decision. We need to keep in mind that a low NAV does not always provide us with the scope of high returns!

PROFESSIONALS SHOULD PLAN THEIR INVESTMENT WITH A VISION

During a recent visit to Assam, a host of professional friends and readers of my newspaper column asked me how they could plan their investments without loosing their principal. I was happy to tell them that they should invest with a vision. We should all plan our investments meticulously. This group of readers that I am referring to were in their mid-forties and their children had already grown up. Now it was necessary for them to plan for their children's higher education, take care of family security, organize their pensions and build their houses.

I was pleasantly surprised to find that most people in the group had already built their own houses. This is the best thing any professional can do. This group included well-known doctors, a few very successful advocates, prize-winning film makers, and very popular writer-cum-editors of newspapers. Another remarkable detail was that all the spouses were also working. However, despite being in such privileged positions they had not planned their investments. A few of them had not even taken the benefit of income tax relief which they are officially entitled to for paying a home loan to the bank.

During the course of our discussions I did advise them that if they availed of all the tax benefits they were entitled to, then their finances would further improve. They could then save that amount for the education of their children. One of the couples, both doctors, had taken out a large home loan and their EMI was very high. They were repaying such a large amount to the bank that it was difficult for them to save money for the education of their son. They realized that if he somehow secured a seat in an IIM, it would be difficult for them to manage his expenditure. (Nowadays, the fee in IIM is very high and it will go further up in days to come).

The couple had taken a housing loan a few years back @12% interest in the name of the husband only, though the wife was also earning. They were unaware that if the loan had been taken in both their names, it would have been possible for both of them to claim a much bigger tax benefit. My suggestion to them was to pre-close the loan and reapply for another home loan in both their names as a few nationalized banks were giving home loans @8% interest.

Needless to say, if someone takes Rs. 20 lakhs as a home loan for twenty years @12% interest then they would end up paying around Rs. 60 lakhs by the end of the term. But if they took a home loan @9% interest, they would end up paying only Rs. 31 lakh or less. My sincere suggestion to my friends and readers is to take a loan in the name of both husband and wife if both are working or if both of them have separate files for earned income.

It was a revelation to me that around 60% of the professionals did not know the benefit of having a PPF account. I advised them to open an account and start saving a minimum of Rs. 500 or a maximum of Rs. 1 lakh per annum. One of my doctor readers stated that they did not know how to handle cash that they received daily from their patients. I told them that these were not ill-gotten gains, so they needed to pay income tax as due and save the balance money in an arbitrage fund (without any income tax). With the last amendment, the income tax slab has gone down. After availing all IT benefits if the taxable income stands at Rs. 2 lakhs or less, they are exempt from paying taxes. Between Rs. 2-5 lakhs a taxpayer need to pay 10%, and the amount exceeding Rs. 8 lakhs is taxed at 20%.

The most important thing is to plan ahead of time. This is the time to invest in equity under SIP. Considering an age of 45 years, 55% of their investment should be in equity and the rest in fixed income, like Bank FD, Post Office FD, PPF, Deferred Annuity Scheme, etc. Money has no value of its own till someone adds value to it. Rip Van Winkle kept one thousand pounds to enjoy his life but it failed to support him for even a month when he woke up!

KEEP YOUR INVESTMENTS SIMPLE

The year 2008 saw a bloodbath on bourses all over the world. The fear of losing brought down the Indian market to a pre-2006 level. Naturally, investors panicked. At that time, it was difficult for even RBI to revive the market. The steps taken by RBI were to ensure that liquidity improved and inflation dropped. Over the next couple of years, the market has rebounded and is once again performing well. In fact, the emerging economies of Brazil, Russia, India, and China weathered the recession much better than the developed economies in Europe, U.S., and Japan.

At that time in the midst of this financial massacre, I was pleasantly surprised to receive a call from a lady executive in Digboi who asked me about the best shares she could buy during such a fall. It was clear that this lady investor of Assam had matured. She bought shares of BHEL and Reliance Industries and wanted to buy more. She also invested only fifty percent of her savings in equity and that too in a systematic way. Yes, it is always prudent to keep the investment horizon simple, especially for investors from the Northeast as most of you have entered this arena recently. Of course, the mutual fund companies would try to attract investors under various new names and brands. Do not depend totally on the brokers. Talk to a financial advisor of your choice with an open heart. He will advise you about the newly launched funds. Try to do your own homework. Study investment magazines and books worth their name and decide for yourself what you want to do. People earn money with great effort. They have a responsibility to protect their hard-earned money. If investors do not care for their money, no one will manage it well for them. Long back, Kautilya explained that it was not enough to just earn money, it was necessary to save it for the future. But even more important is to protect the hard-earned wealth. This dictum of protection from the past should be followed by every investor at all costs even now. The share market directly or indirectly reflects the state of the economy. The international markets are passing through a difficult time. Everyone should think well before investing. You should invest in equity only if you can spare money for not less than five years. The Indian market has recovered, but is still volatile and investors will have to take a calculated risk. But keep in mind that this is one of the best times for investing.

Recently, Raja Deka (named changed) wrote to me that he invested in at least sixteen mutual funds, but he lost money in all of them except two funds! He was desperate to know what could be done. He also bought shares of Himachal futuristic and lost an enormous amount of money. He wanted to know how he could recover that loss. I felt very sorry after studying his portfolio. It is almost impossible to salvage such a situation. It was actually really bad. I, however, advised him that some of the funds which he subscribed to were good. He should not only be able to get back the lost money but also be able to make a decent profit in due course of time. He needed to be patient. But some of his shares and funds were beyond retrieval. Either he could continue to carry his baggage till a decent up-turn happened or he could retire the loss now and enter into large cap shares like L&T, Reliance Industry, or buy NIFTY Index and diversified mutual funds like HSBC Equity, DSPML Equity 100, etc.

It has now been proven beyond any doubt that money management depends on the level of your financial literacy. Monika Halan, executive editor of *Money* made a bold statement in one of her articles that financial literacy will soon be the buzz word in India. It is interesting to note that financial product manufacturers, regulators, and stock exchanges have identified the lack of financial literacy as a key roadblock in the conversion of savings into investment. This trend is more pronounced in Northeast India where people have a high proportion of small savings but are still unaware about how it should be converted into an asset class of equity. I strongly recommend all educated people to read the article in the "Last Note" of *Money* magazine from 10th September, 2008. (www.outlookmoney.com)

I have already mentioned FMPs (Fixed Maturity Plans). Mutual fund houses now aggressively introduce and market fixed maturity plans. Equity linked FMPs in turn invest primarily in equity linked debentures and securitized debt instruments. These are highly sophisticated yet complex structured products. Most of our investors are new and need not be exposed to a complex product. I have noticed that when misfortune befalls a new investor and they feel beaten once, they shy away from the investment horizon itself. That would be unfortunate. I feel that the new investor should be helped to choose simple investment tools like PPF, Diversified Mutual Fund, ELSS, Liquid Fund, Arbitrage Fund and Bank Fixed Deposits. Let them mature slowly and graduate to more complex products later, on their own.

CHAPTER TWO

The Power of Fixed Income

SAVINGS IN BANK & POST OFFICE SCHEMES

Small savings are not really small. They are like raindrops. A trickle creates lakes, rivers, and with time, the sea. I had mentioned before that a friend of mine, who lives near Ugratra Temple of Guwahati, quit smoking on the advice of his doctor. He used to spend around Rs. 50 per day on cigarettes. His wife, a teacher in a college at Guwahati, requested him to allow her to save this amount in a small-savings scheme. My friend agreed and started handing over Rs. 50 per day to his wife from April 1980. She went to a post office and met a lady who was the former Director of a small-savings organization. On her advice she opened a PPF account and started depositing the amount—Rs. 1500—religiously every month.

When she retired in 2005 and went to check the balance. She found Rs. 20 lakhs in her account! I am sure we can safely assume that it was a pleasant surprise. She did not withdraw any of the money and started depositing more every month. This gave her the advantage of a tax benefit under section 80C and her entire interest earned also became tax free. Today she uses the account almost like a savings bank account. Every year, in April, she withdraws Rs. 1 lakh 80 thousand, which automatically gets replaced over the year. She is happy, comfortable, and secure in her retirement. Surely, young wives and working daughters and sons can follow her example.

Once upon a time, in Assam, discussing money matters with parents was considered rude and uncivilized. The atmosphere has now changed. Nowadays, the younger generation actually tries to educate their guardians about the opportunities available to save and invest in the country. There are a few small savings schemes which offer section 80C tax benefits. These schemes are:

1. National Savings Certificate Scheme: 8% interest per annum without limit for tenures of six years.
2. Public Provident Fund Scheme, 8% interest per annum with a limit of Rs. 1 lakh annually for tenures of 15 years.

The interest accrued in the PPF does not attract any Income tax. All other small saving schemes are not tax exempt. Despite tax implications, three schemes are very popular with the public. These are: (a) Monthly Income Scheme of Post Office: (6 years tenure) with 8% return; (b) Kisan Vikas Patra: (money doubles in 8 years and 7 months) with 8.41% return; (c) Senior Citizen Savings Scheme: (5 years tenure, minimum age 55) with 9% return. During the year 2006-7 bank fixed deposit accounts were very popular when some of the banks offered 9% to 10% interest. There are a few others schemes in the post office and banks which provide 80C benefit, like PPF and ELSS.

Till now, Senior Citizen Schemes and long term bank fixed deposits with a higher rate of interest (9-10% returns) without income tax benefit were good for retired persons. But with an inflation rate of almost 8%, they have lost their earlier shine. Still, inflation is a temporary phenomenon and it is always our hope that it will reduce with proper corrective measures. For a retired person, security and safety are two important requirements. I strongly feel that anyone 75 years and above should keep away from equity investments and may depend for their monthly expenses on Pension Benefit, Bank Fixed Deposit, SCSS (Senior Citizens Saving Scheme) and PPF. In fact, for our senior years, PPF is the most lucrative and meaningful scheme. I have no hesitation to recommend that every working woman and man should start investing in PPF from their youth. This is one of the best schemes for a single mothers, young widows, private medical practitioners and advocates. It is most appropriate for artists, singers, theatre artists and journalists who do not have regular salaries and pension. One thing must be kept in mind that small-savings schemes are habit forming. It develops an attitude for saving. Once people feel comfortable with small-savings schemes they will later be able to comfortably graduate to mutual funds and then to the share market.

FIXED DEPOSITS & DEBT FUNDS SUIT SENIOR CITIZENS BEST

"What is the best saving instrument for us now," a worried senior citizen asked his friend. "I am worried myself. How do I advice you?" replied his friend. Both of them decided to visit one of their chartered accountant friends for his advice. All three sat together over an evening cup of tea in the chamber of Mr. Hazarika, who was also a specialist in taxes and investments.

Mr. Hazarika advised them that senior citizens above 70 need not invest in equity unless their risk-taking capacity is high. The volatility of the share market is unpredictable. So people dependent on a regular income out of their investment generally should not invest in equity or equity-related instruments. Both friends asked him what senior citizens like them should do.

Mr. Hazarika said that all the investable funds available should be distributed to fixed and fluctuating-income instruments like Bank Fixed Deposit; debt instruments like Debt Fund, Gilt Fund, Liquid Fund or an Equity Based Arbitrage Fund, depending on tax-paying factors. Both friends became awestruck and conceded that they had not heard much about Arbitrage Funds, Gilt Funds and Debt Funds. They were only vaguely aware of a Bond Fund of the Reserve Bank of India which no longer existed. Mr. Hazarika advised them that senior citizens must learn more about investment avenues. Inflation can cut away more than thirty percent of income. This must be protected. What is to be done now?

Mr. Hazarika asked whether both of them are tax-paying citizens or not. Both replied in the affirmative. "In that event it would be appropriate for you to divide your investment into two segments. First, invest at least sixty-eight percent of your investable amount in a Bank Fixed Deposit and the balance in tax-saving instruments."

"Why sixty eight percent? Why not sixty or fifty percent?" asked one of the friends. "Because you are sixty eight years old and you are still capable of taking some risk. We are deciding on the premise that there should be no more equity exposure from the seventieth year only."

"Oh! We understand your reasoning now!"

"But it is not necessary that you have to invest in equity at all! If you are still risk averse, you can keep all your money in debt instruments from now onward. But that will give you limited returns of 10-12% in total. Both friends unanimously agreed that they could subscribe at least 10% of their investment in equity for they needed to beat inflation. Hazarika advised them that in that case they could keep 5% of their investment in a balanced fund. The next obvious question: Which balanced fund to subscribe? "Go to valueresearchonline. com and you can subscribe to any five-star or four-star fund. You can consult moneycontrolonline.com also. But my preference is value-research. It is an independent, honest, and valuable advisory," said Hazarika.

Since 73% of your investable funds have been taken care of, now the balance 27% should be deployed. Out of this 27%, if you have an existing PPF account, you can keep 7% there up to a maximum of Rs. 100,000, And you can invest the balance 20% in the IDFC long-term bond fund or in the ICICI Gilt Fund. These are not taxable and give a return of 13% to 20% percent at present. Alternatively, you can keep the amount in an Arbitrage Fund with no tax and with returns of around 8-11% all the time. You should know that during the last and still continuing financial crisis, when equity tumbled down to—50%, the only funds that withstood the turmoil were Bond Funds, Gilt Funds, and Arbitrage Funds. The returns of Bond and Gilt Funds may decrease if the interest rate stop going down or if it comes up. But Arbitrage Funds hold their own irrespective of a meltdown. You can have faith on this fund. It is an all-weather friend of senior citizens with no tax impact.

THE BEST TIME TO TEACH CHILDREN
THE VALUE OF MONEY

A lot of mail was received from our readers during the month asking for the best time to teach their wards about the value of money. Some of the young parents mentioned that in their family, discussions about the family silver, wealth, and money earned by a parent were never discussed. In fact, it was considered bad manners if children tried to take part in money matters of the family. Children were expected to study and play and parent always needed to fend for them. But the perception has changed in the twenty first century. It is now required that children should know the value of money early in life. Now the question arises: How early should children start hands-on training on money management?

It is now felt that children should have hands-on experience of handling money from an early age. Why? It is because the requirement of money has multiplied. Lifestyles of people have undergone a tremendous change. Life on earth has become competitive. This competitiveness has increased the necessity of money. Earnings have not multiplied, but expenses have gone up exponentially. In Assam, the marriage of a daughter was not a very expensive affair. Today, it has changed. In the latter half of the 20th century, the birth of a child was celebrated with an offering to God and feeding *paramanna* to all the neighbours. Today, a birthday is a big affair and enormously costly. The expectations of children have also gone up. If children are allowed to have hands-on experience of handling money, they would at least get an opportunity to learn the value of money. So, what is an appropriate time to introduce the concept of money in the lives of children?

This is not an easy question. Different societies have different approaches to money. Children are allowed to handle money from early childhood in Rajasthan, MP, and UP. But in south India and in northeast India, children handle money only after going to college. However, many parents are now forced to talk openly to their children as money has become a major family issue due to price rise, non-availability of cash flow due to recession, pay cuts, and job losses. According to a recent survey by the T. Rowe Price group, nearly half of the parents of school-going children have used the recession as a catalyst to talk about money with their children.

Question: When should children be allowed to handle money? Answer: As soon as children start to explore the outside world. According to an expert on child psychology, children should be introduced to money matters as soon as s/he develops a want for any product or object like toys, chocolates, books, etc. What should be the age? Children start demanding when they are between three-four years of age. This would also be the right age to introduce them to money. Till this age children feel that whatever they desire simply materialize. They develop a desire and it gets fulfilled. How it gets fulfilled is not their concern. According to experts in child psychology, this is the time that a healthy outlook needs to be developed in a child.

Indian parents are very hesitant to talk about money with their children. Parents feel that just like sex education, money education should start in school. This is an inherent hesitation of Indian parents. According to Laura Levine, an expert on financial literacy, "Parents feel they are not qualified. But kids learn most of their money lessons best from their parents. You just need to talk about it." Really, experts agree, that it is not hard if you take it step-by-step. "The best way to introduce the concept of money management is to give children some money to manage," said Janet Bodnar, author of the world-famous book "Raising Money-Smart Kids." What is the advice of Bodnar?

Bodnar suggests setting a weekly allowance that equates to half the age of children at the rate of $2 for a four year old and $5 when a child hits the 10th year. According to me, for Indian parents there need not be any particular formula to be followed on the amount. Parents can simply shift some money that they were spending monthly for the children's toys, snacks, storybooks, etc. and allow them to decide how to spend it. The most important thing is for the child to see that managing money is all about making choices. If you buy one expensive thing you will not have money to buy another. It is like teaching children about healthy eating. You do not force children to taste from a food pyramid—rather you cook for them to experience it. Likewise, parents need to make money experiences a part of their child's living. Perhaps this would help children realise the value of saving. Of course, a guardian has to be strict about the amount to be paid each week or month.

N.R. Srinivasan, an astute accountant, started giving his teenaged son Rs. 10/—every day and asked him to divide this allowance into three parts at the rate of Rs. 3/—each for his T-shirts, CDs, Tiffin, and the balance of one rupee for daily saving to buy whatever he wanted—like an extra pair of shoes, socks, or a cap. The formula developed in him a sense of saving and respect for the value of money. In later years, his son grew up to become an investment expert after completing his MBA.

Mr. Srinivasan's friend, Bibek Talukdar, gave his young son, Paban, whatever he wanted. He even yielded to Paban's demand for a pair of shoes that cost Rs. 4000, whereas he himself was wearing a pair that cost Rs. 800 only. He never taught his son the value of money. When Paban was in the last year of college, he demanded a motorbike from his father. When his father refused, Paban insolently wanted to know why he was given birth if his father was so incompetent to meet his needs. He threatened to commit suicide to save face and for the loss of prestige in front of his classmates. Ultimately, his father once again yielded and had to agree. In his later years, this young man became a vagabond. According to experts, it is the parents who can inculcate the best money habits in children by their deeds.

In case parents do want their children to become money savvy, then let them start with a simple piggybank. This will develop the concept of *spend, save, and share* early in life. This concept should be started with kids early to prevent an enormously frustrating habit that many of them develop: In every store, shop, exhibition, and mall they will harp and whine "Give me, give me, give me . . . !"

As the children reach adolescence they should be introduced to banking procedures and as soon as they pass out of the high school they need to be introduced to credit cards. Many of our children now leave home for college. Knowing how to use a credit card or debit card will help them mange their finances while in the hostel. Parents can deposit money in their children's account in their local bank and they can withdraw the money in the town where they live . . . Delhi, Pune, Bangalore, Chennai, or elsewhere.

In my opinion, parents need to explain to their teenaged children that money is a tool that provides both enjoyment and security when used wisely. Srinivasan once told me that his grandfather grew up poor and was never able to enjoy his money. Srinivasan himself was fortunate to grow up affluent and lacked awareness of the cost and value of money when young. He wants his son, Hari, to have respect for money but not love it too much or fear it too much. A healthy attitude towards money would make his son a balanced human being—that is what is needed in life, he thought.

All parents must remember the words of Einstein that the mystery of the compounding of money is far more complex to him than the complexity of the laws of universe. Ask your four year old child to save Rs. 5/—per day in a bank and ask him to count the sum when he is sixty years old. It will be difficult for him to count the number of zeros. A recession is a great time for you to introduce the concepts of money management to your child, for only then can you feel the real pinch and power of money.

CHILDREN MUST BE TAUGHT THE VALUE OF MONEY

We have grown up in an atmosphere of command economy. During our younger days all the important decisions of our life were taken by our parents. What we will be when we grow up was also decided by our parents. The decision whether to pursue Arts, Commerce, or Science was also taken in large measure by our parents. Whether a young child would be a doctor, an advocate, or an IAS officer was mainly dependent on our parents. We had almost no say in creating and shaping our life. In fact, during our childhood and thereafter we were scared of our parents. Times have changed. Now parents are scared of their children. Young children now have the attitude and aptitude to decide their future. Yet, children are still unaware and not taught about the value of wealth creation or to develop the habit of saving by their parents. This needs to be done. Nowadays, even in school, children are taken out to the market and taught how to spend money, how to make a budget, and how to save money. But the best education on wealth creation should come from the guardian or parents at home.

Use real-life experiences to demonstrate everything you want to teach. Learning by observing and doing is the most powerful tool. Such as when you go grocery shopping, and can use the opportunity to showcase planned spending, or how to recognise value for money. If you decide to use a credit card at a restaurant, you can show your child how a credit card works, when it can be used, and how to calculate a tip! Why are the children of industrialists so much more money savvy from childhood? This is essentially because they are taught the value of money at the dinner table. The best time to teach the value of money to children is at the dinner table and while on holidays. The mothers of most industrialists taught them how to make their family budget. In our families, budgeting is never done. Money is spent as it comes. Times have changed and the practice of budgeting should now be taught and practised in our families.

How important is it to teach your children about money, its place, and its value? Considering that money does, in a lot of ways, make the world go round, you might think it one of life's obvious lessons, gained through experience. Or you might assume that money management is tackled in school. Think again. Arming your child with the right attitude and necessary skills at the right time will afford them with the greatest possible advantage: the opportunity and power to make decisions.

How and when to discuss with children the values of money? This is one of the toughest challenges that parents now days face. Educating, motivating, and empowering children to become regular savers and investors will enable them to keep more of the money they earn and do more with the money they spend.

Discuss money openly. So many parents do not discuss finances within the family either because it is considered inappropriate, or personal. Consider this: If you don't actively provide the correct information to your child, how is s/he to know, understand and inculcate your values? Therefore, as soon as your child can count, introduce her/him to money. Observation and repetition are two important ways in which children learn. As they grow older, have frank discussions about how to save it, how to make it grow, and how to spend it wisely.

We need to help our children to distinguish between needs and wants. These are habits that die hard, and influence how your child will approach money and its place in her/his life. If they can differentiate between need-to-have and nice-to-have, then they're halfway to a solid and secure future.

It is imperative to help our children set their own goals. If it's a toy that they must have, then regard this as a good opportunity to teach the child how to be responsible with money, and prioritise between what they want, and mindless spending. This would help develop the concept of a family budget. Allow your child to make spending decisions, which means that they will learn from the choices they make. And learn that it's to their advantage to do a little homework before buying, waiting for the right time to buy, and actually deciding if the product selected is what they really want.

As children step into their teenage years at thirteen, it would be great to take them to a bank and open a joint account with a parent. Take them to an ATM when you withdraw money and explain how it works. Begin simply, though your parents may or may not have done, with a piggy bank. If you do give your child an allowance, get them to set aside a small portion of it every time. Explain and demonstrate the concept of earning interest income on savings. Provide an incentive: offer to match what your child saves on his/her own. While paying your child in instalments, you can use 12 envelopes; 1 for each month with a larger envelope to hold all the envelopes for the year. Encourage your children to save receipts from all purchases in the envelopes and keep notes on what they do with their money.

Children always learn by observing how their parents keep, record, and spend money. So we need to be an example for the family. You can use every opportunity to demonstrate planned spending and healthy habits of using debit and credit cards. Do not forget to remind them that credit card payments must be made immediately and that a credit card should not be given to anyone, not even to their mothers!

You can teach your child that spending money can be fun and very productive when spending is well-planned, and that a penny saved is indeed a penny earned! Take your children to the post office and show them how you saved your initial money in a post office account. Take them to a bank and explain the difference between a credit card and a debit card. The world is changing fast. If you do not teach your children the value of money, the world will keep evolving and your kids will not only remain ignorant but actually fall behind. Would you really like this to happen to your children?

SENIOR CITIZENS SAVING SCHEME IS A GREAT STEP TODAY

A large number of senior citizen readers have written to us asking whether the Government of India's SCSS (Senior Citizens Saving Scheme) has been withdrawn or is it still in vogue. Are investments in the scheme still profitable for retired persons even now?

I would like to emphatically state that for any retired person, as of date, SCSS is one of the best schemes to invest in, especially during the present time when all the banks have lowered interest rates on deposits. Some senior citizens cannot decide where to invest their money on maturity. One lady wrote that she stayed invested for last three years in a Nationalized Bank with an annual return of 9.5%. On maturity of the FD Certificate the same bank is offering her a much lower rate of interest bringing down her annual income. She wanted to know where she could invest with a higher interest rate. Another gentleman was told by the bank that the senior citizens scheme with a higher interest has been withdrawn. This is not true. The Government of India's scheme is still in vogue and it is the best scheme going in the market for retired persons.

SCSS is often referred to as the best alternative for the elderly to invest their money. Is this justified? Here is a detailed look at all the features of the Senior Citizen Savings Scheme, and an analysis of whether you should invest in it or not.

Investment in SCSS can only be made by people 60 years of age or above. People who have retired on superannuation or under a voluntary retirement scheme can also invest if they are at least 55 years old. The account can be opened as a single account, or can be opened in joint names. The joint account holder can only be the spouse. There is no age limit applicable for the joint account holder (spouse). In case of the death of the primary account holder, the spouse can continue the account—this is subject to the condition that his/her total investment in SCSS should not exceed Rs. 15 lakhs. People retiring from the defence services are eligible to invest in the scheme irrespective of any age limit, but there are some additional conditions that apply.

An SCSS account can be opened only by individuals. It cannot be opened by Non-Resident Indians (NRIs), Persons of Indian Origin (PIOs), and Hindu Undivided Families (HUFs). For people between 55 and 60 years of age, the amount invested in SCSS has to come from their retirement benefits. For persons over the age of 60 years, there is no restriction on the source of funds invested. SCSS has a maturity of 5 years, which is extendable by 3 years. The rate of interest offered on the investment is 9% per annum and the account can be opened in post offices or in nationalised banks. Perhaps, ICICI is the only private sector bank that handles SCSS. There is a Section 80C income tax benefit on the investments made in SCSS, but there is no income tax benefit on the interest earned from it. Investments made on or after 1st April, 2008 are deductible from your income under section 80C of the Income Tax Act. The interest earned on the deposit is fully taxable.

The income tax applicable is deducted at source. If your income is not taxable, you can provide form 15H or 15G so that no tax is deducted at source. The tax is deducted at source only if the total interest in a year is over Rs. 5,000. The interest is paid out every 3 months. This means that SCSS can provide a steady, periodic income. There is no provision for cumulative income. The SCSS is backed by the Government of India, and thus, carries a sovereign guarantee for principal and interest payments. Therefore, it is among the safest investment avenues available in India.

One reader has asked that if he wanted to invest more than 15 lakh, where he should invest. My recommendation would be, without taking any risk, a Monthly Income Plan with Bonus from the post office. But you must remember that if you look for absolute safety, a time will come when your money value will deplete so far that it may not be possible to even buy potatoes. If you have a sizable amount of money, invest some in equity also to take care of inflation. Since the scheme is absolutely safe, and provides periodic payment of interest, retirees and senior citizens can invest a portion of their retirement corpus in the Senior Citizen Savings Scheme.

A PAN CARD HAS BECOME A NECESSITY
FOR ALL INCOME EARNERS

Perhaps every citizen now knows that a budget from a few years back included a provision that any person investing money in a fixed deposit is required to quote their PAN (Permanent Account Number). This provision is applicable to all persons irrespective of the fact whether he or she is an income tax payer or not. In fact, banks have been advised to deduct money if no PAN is quoted even by non-income tax payers. In case the wrong PAN is provided by depositors, there will be a 20% deduction of tax as a penalty. Till recently a PAN card was a necessity for income tax payers who submitted income tax returns annually. Nowadays, the PAN card is necessary for buying a car or any big purchase, owning a cell phone number and now to open a Fixed Deposit account in a bank even if you are not a tax payer.

A few years ago a PAN card was also necessary to travel abroad. It was necessary for those travellers to submit IT (Income Tax) returns even if they were not income tax payers. (It was necessary for such people to submit a nil return). While submitting the nil return they had to quote their PAN. This provision was abolished a few years back. Now a PAN card is required for any kind of financial transaction. The matter of obtaining a PAN card for individuals has gained importance now because irrespective of the total income (more or less than the taxable income), if a person keeps money in a bank's fixed deposit account s/ he would be required to have a PAN card. This has now become law. I would therefore like to recommend that all people wishing to invest money in a bank or elsewhere should apply for a PAN card. What is a PAN card? I will try to make it simple. PAN is the abbreviation of Permanent Account Number. Actually this is a unique number allotted to individuals or corporate entities by the Department of Income Tax, Government of India. It is more like an identification number. A PAN card is a plastic laminated photo-ID card that contains a unique alphanumeric number and mentions the applicant's name, father's name, date of birth, signature, and a logo of the Government of India and Department of Income Tax. By default, a PAN has five letters first, then four digits, and then one letter again. A PAN card is used mainly for the following reasons:

1. Every Indian earning more than the tax free limit must have one and only one PAN card.
2. All FD accounts in banks or non-governmental organizations need the PAN.
3. PAN is needed for all high value purchases, whether payment is by cash, cheque, or credit.
4. It serves as a photo-identity card for all Indian citizens.

With the change in law a PAN has become necessary for everyone who has an FD account, including a widow who may earn an income below the taxable threshold. The threshold limit for payment of income tax for all categories of people has recently been upwardly revised and most of the retired senior citizens and some of their spouses have come out of the income-tax net. However, a widow earning below the threshold limit, even if she has submitted form 15, will be taxed for her fixed deposit savings by the bank if she does not provide a PAN. In certain cases, if PANs are mistakenly quoted, even inadvertently, taxes will be deducted at double the rate. This is where the shoe will pinch for a senior citizen or a surviving spouse. All persons with a bank FD must be very vigilant if they want to avoid unnecessary deductions of tax and penalty fees. This provision will apply to regular salary earners also unless they submit a PAN. Many senior citizens never apply for a PAN card thinking that since they are beyond the ambit of income tax, no PAN card is required. This was a valid argument till a few years ago, but no more. Remember: When it comes to taxes, ignorance cannot be an excuse!

My humble suggestion is not to panic. Only we need to organise the PAN number at the earliest. Having a pan card is very useful and easy. It can be used as a photo identity card also besides using it for all financial transactions. This number is actually issued by the income tax department to track any financial transactions and also to ensure non-evasion of tax by eligible citizens. The importance of the PAN card will continue till a unique Identification number is issued by the central government to each citizen. The project has already been taken up recently. A few persons recently wrote to me asking as to how and where to apply for a PAN card?

The Income Tax Department has authorised UTI Investor Services Limited to manage and issue PAN cards for smooth processing. I must admit that the processing is far from smooth; however, it does eventually get done. You can approach one of the many PAN-card processing centres that have mushroomed across different localities or you can apply online through their website for an application form. There is a specific form and that needs to be filled to enable UTI Investor Services Limited to issue a PAN card with your photograph. A small fee is also charged for the convenience. PAN cards can also be issued to NRIs and is essential for them to conduct any financial transactions within the country.

SAVING HABITS OF WOMEN NEED EMPOWERMENT

During the twenty-first century, more women are working than in the last century. Nowadays, women are heading organizations like PepsiCo, HSBC bank, HDFC bank, and Coca Cola. Many women have become successful lawyers, doctors, advocates, and teachers. With women occupying such senior positions, their incomes have increased dramatically and it is natural for them to save more and more. But this has not happened. A recently conducted survey surprisingly revealed that women are better spenders than savers. Women spend more on their family than on themselves. But this habit needs to reversed, because children idolize their mother rather than their father. They no doubt keep the father in high esteem but children are generally scared of their fathers and friendly with their mothers. It is really a myth that sons are closer to the mother and daughters are closer to the father. Why do women spend more money rather than saving? This emanates from the feeling that she is the natural guardian of the family. Any shortfall in the budget and lifestyle is picked up by the working mother rather than the father. Even in the office, it is found that female employees do not hesitate to buy lunch for colleagues compared to male employees. Such are the adverse effects of natural benevolence.

Many studies have shown that women lag behind men in saving for retirement. In a 2008 survey of more than 1,300 workers or retirees over age 25 by the non-partisan Employee Benefit Research Institute (EBRI) and Matthew Greenwald & Associates, 68% of women and 76% of men said that they "had" saved for retirement; 59% of women and 70% of men said they were currently saving; and 58% of women and 64% of men said they were contributing to a workplace retirement account. Two recent studies of participants in large-company plans show similar results. This is not only the case in India. Even in America women save less than men. Vanguard, a mutual fund company that also manages retirement plans in the USA, reported that in 2007 the average account balance of more than three million participants in their 401(k) plans was $56,723 for women, compared with $95,447 for men. More recently, Hewitt Associates consultants surveyed nearly 2 million participants in the large-company 401(k) plans that the company manages and found that women had an average of $56,320 in their accounts, compared with over $100,000 for men.

This is the time that our society needs to empower women so that they can save better for the rainy days. Working single women need to think specifically about thrifty saving habits. Saving in banks or in government plans are the safest option but that will not support them fully due to inflationary pressures. A women who could manage their monthly budget with Rs. 10,000 per month a decade back finds it almost impossible to carry on unless she can earn more than double the amount. This is the effect of inflation.

Potatoes, which used to cost Rs. 3/kg now cost Rs. 28/kg. What is the way out? If she would have kept all her savings in a nationalised bank, her money would have been safe alright but now she would have had to depend on borrowed money or on the alms of others. Fortunately, she kept a portion of her money in a mutual fund that gave her a return of 25% of money saved. Every single woman and single mother must keep it in mind that the protection of your assets is not enough. The asset must be capable of providing inflation adjusted return for at least twenty years. What should women do? They need to invest and save early and judiciously. Where do women need to invest? Investment in EPF is a must. Those who do not have EPF should surely start saving in PPF from the beginning of their career. PPF can be started with Rs. 500 per annum. Investment in PPF will not be enough. To beat inflation it will be mandatory for a person to invest first in mutual funds. Investment in mutual funds is not as safe as a bank fixed deposit. But women must learn to take a little risk if they want to afford a better lifestyle.

Which are the mutual funds they need to select and how long do they need to keep investing? It would be prudent to study a few investment journals. Many may not be able to do so. In that case, they need to approach a well-known bank. Most banks have their own investment desk. SBI has an appointed person to help clients with investment advice. Similarly, Standard Chartered has its own investment advisor. These advisors may be able to guide new investors. I would highly recommend that all investors should try to study the websites moneycontrol.com and valueresearch.com and invest in four-star and five-star mutual funds. Women above forty-five years of age should be able to reduce risk buy avoiding fully diversified equity funds. They need to subscribe at least sixty percent of their savings in a debt fund.

Alternatively they can opt for a balanced fund so that the risk can be divided. Single mothers have a greater responsibility towards their children. It would be prudent to subscribe to insurance policies so that their children are not handicapped in case of an emergent situation. Education and marriage are two important components of life. In order to sail smoothly, a single mother must plan for the correct ULIP policies. Of late, India has started great ULIP policies though they are costly compared to investment plans of mutual funds. ULIP policies should be subscribed to after learning all the details of the plan. Each policy tries to be different. Being different is not the solution. It should be cost effective for the subscriber . . . in this case, a working single mother.

CHAPTER THREE

Investments, Income Tax, and the Single Parent

IMPACT OF INCOME TAX ON THE MIDDLE CLASS

May is the best time to plan for a reduction of income tax for the current year. Many people do not want to concede that during the last three years, income tax on the middle class has come down considerably. It is a recorded fact. Though the recent budgets have not been able to inspire many investors and corporate entities, yet it has brought in certain changes in respect to personal taxes. It has also brought in a new dimension to the New Pension Scheme which is meant now for the common people of India. The impact of these two measures is far reaching. It is important to discuss the implications of these two measures for the benefit of the tax payers. Nowadays, tax payers are able to pay income tax through ATMs also. The Corporation Bank started the facility first and all other banks will surely follow the system soon.

In what could be a major relief to income-tax payers, the Government of India is proposing to impose only a 10% tax up to an income of Rest. 10 lakh. Now, this is a proposal only for public discourse. I hope that the Direct Tax Code becomes a law replacing the IT Act of 1961. In that event, the middle class will be greatly benefited. This subject needs a detailed discussion that is done in a separate article later.

However, it should be noted that the Government of India desires that all the persons, who do not have to pay any income tax, shall also have to submit" KYC "(PAN CARD AND PROOF OF RSIDENCE) to bank or any other authority, in case they have any interest earnings from Fixed Deposit. Till recently no senior citizen, who do not have taxable income; have to submit details of pan card to the bank or any other organization where money is kept in Fixed Deposit.

Despite the criticism of opposition parties against the low benefits of income tax, in actual practice over last few years, personal income tax has come down considerably. During the year ending March 2008, people earning above Rs. 3 lakhs annually paid an income tax of around Rs. 50,000.00 after availing all concessions. During the year ending March 2009, the tax was around Rs. 20,000 only for the same annual income. Since then, if they maintain the same level of earning or a little more and handle their savings carefully, they might be able to take themselves out of the personal income tax ambit completely. With a heavy reduction in taxes, their real income went up in 2009-10 despite the inflationary effect, for the first time in many years. Many people are not realising this effect due to the high cost of commodities.

The recent budget has good benefits for salaried persons whose annual salary is above Rs. 10,00,000. Nowadays, most of the senior executives earn an income around that figure. Gone are the days when a Vice President or a General Manger would get Rs. 50,000/—per month. Now Executive Directors, General Mangers, Senior General Mangers, Vice Presidents and Presidents get upwards of Rs. 85,000 per month and more. From a few years back they have not had to pay any surcharge on their earned income, which adds an additional benefit of around Rs. 3 lakh per year. This is a great benefit to a salaried person.

Senior citizens will also be happy that the exemption limit on their taxable income has been enhanced. Earlier, senior citizens did not pay tax if their annual income was within Rs. 2,25,000 per annum. That meant that a senior citizen with a monthly income of Rs. 19,000 had to pay income tax. Now, senior citizens are not required to pay income tax even if their earning is Rs. 20,000 per month or Rs. 2,40,000 annually. If these seniors can save around Rs. 1 lakh under 80C, they are not required to pay tax even if they earn a little over Rs. 28,000 per month. This means that some of the retired judges, retired senior bureaucrats, and retired General Managers from both public and private sector undertakings will avoid taxation as most of their pensions are around this limit. Naturally, senior citizens are happy about this.

In many cases where both husband and wife were working and are now retired as senior citizens, they would also be in a better financial position than before. A chart is given below to show how the new budget has benefited the senior citizens.

It is now apparent that earlier the tax liability for senior citizens earning Rs. 2,40,000 was Rs. 1545/—annually. Now they will not have to pay any tax if their income remained the same. Only with an income of Rs. 3 lakh will they be liable to pay an annual tax of Rs. 6,180/—or around five hundred rupees per month.

As on 2013 there is no separate exemption limit of income tax for ladies. Now, men and women have the same exemption limit of Rs 2 lakh per annum.

It is quite apparent that no lady shall have to pay any income tax if her earning is around Rs. 2,00,000 per annum or around Rs. 17,000 per month. If they can save money under 80C they will not be required to pay income tax even if they earn Rs. 3,00,000 per annum or Rs. 24,000 per month. This would mean that most government officials and midlevel private—and public-sector executives will hardly be required to pay any taxes. The new SDCs, Police Officers, Extra Assistant Commissioners, and Executive Engineers drawing around Rs. 25,000 per month will not be required to pay any income tax if their savings are planned properly under 80C.

It is now absolutely clear that a male income-tax payer would have to pay no income tax till his earning exceeds Rs 2,00,000 annually. If the same person can save money under section 80C of the IT Act, they will not have to pay any taxes even if they earn Rs. 300,000 annually or little above Rs. 25,000 per month.

I strongly recommend all young employees to save money under NPS for that would give them the best benefit in the future. We should not think only of today. With proper savings, the future will also be brighter for the younger generation. Nowadays, the Pension Scheme is exempt from income tax provided the money taken out of the pension fund is deployed in annuity. This is a good concession which most people have forgotten to notice. I, however, do not recommend that senior citizens make any contribution to NPS. In case they still have an operative PPF account, they should continue contributing there for that would give them the best benefit during their still older years. Nowadays, people generally live beyond eighty-five years. They should plan for that age, especially now that medical care has become so expensive. Modern health scientists have predicted that human mortality in India would further decrease and most people would now live well beyond ninety by 2030. Healthcare will be vital during those years and saving for a healthy body, mind, and soul would be most imperative. If the Direct Tax Code is implemented in due course of time, perhaps the Finance Minister will get the most blessings from the great Indian middleclass.

IMPACT OF THE DIRECT TAX CODE ON COMMON PEOPLE

A few years back, the Finance Minister announced the proposal of a Direct Tax Code effective April 2011. The Bill is still being discussed, amended, and debated in the Budget Session now in 2013, but once passed, it aims at a comprehensive reform in the sphere of personal and corporate taxation. We will, however, limit our discussion to its impact on common people. To safeguard the interests of business, industry, and workmen, there are number of Chambers of Commerce and Trade Unions. But no organizations exist to protect the interests of regular self-employed and retired people. The Code is open for public discourse, hence it should be studied, debated, discussed, and recommendations should be sent to the Ministry of Finance.

There is a great difference between "Code" and "Act". The government is trying to bring in the Direct Tax Code instead of the present system of Tax under Finance Act. The Code will be a permanent affair like the CrPC or IPC. Once the tax act is converted into a code, it will generally not be necessary to introduce changes every year along with budget. This is a reform that the government wants to bring in for the good of the people. The code does not propose any change in the exemption limit of personal tax. It remains 1,60,000 for men, 1,90,000 for women, and 2,40,000 for senior citizens. Yet, the percentage of taxation has been reduced up to an income of Rs. 10 lakh.

Prima facie, the tax liability will reduce significantly as the draft code proposes to tax incomes up to Rs. 10 lakh at 10%, that between Rs. 10 lakh and Rs. 25 lakh at 20%, and sums in excess of that at 30%. Now, people pay 10% tax only if their income is less than Rs. 3 lakh. A person earning Rs. 10 lakh now pays Rs. 2.11 lakh in taxes. If the Code is implemented, the same person would pay taxes amounting to Rs. 84,000/—only. Is not that really good?

The caveat is that all deductions now available under 80c will vanish! All except a few like new pension schemes, LIC, etc. This means death nails on small-saving schemes. However deductions fewer than 80 C will be enhanced from Rs. 1 lakh to 3 lakh, and this allowance will surely help generation next. Exemptions on retirement benefits will vanish. Retirement savings will become taxable on withdrawal, as the

Draft Code has proposed to usher in exempt-exempt-tax (EET) regime. The PPF and PF will lose all its glamour and tax benefits.

There is a bad news for younger home owners also. The deduction of Rs. 1.5 lakh allowed on interest paid on home loans appears set to be scrapped. There is no mention of such a deduction being allowed in the Draft Code. Young people will not get a tax benefit. On implementation of the Code, all perks will be considered as part of the gross salary for the purpose of taxation. The impact of this provision on the tax liability of an individual will be known only when the rules are published by the income-tax department. But there should be equity in the tax system both vertically and horizontally across all sectors. The tax treatment of perks enjoyed by a government employee and a private sector employee will be the same. Till now the government sector was enjoying a distinct advantage!

It has also been proposed that benefits such as gratuity payments made to employees on change of jobs will be allowed tax exemption only if it is invested in a retirement fund. The most significant reform will be to bring in the EET regime for all approved provident funds, approved superannuation funds, life insurance and the New Pension System trust. The PF and PPF have been under the EEE system. This benefit will vanish. The accumulated amount will be taxed on the year of withdrawal. This will hurt the middle class and, especially, the retirees. However, the proposed code provides that the withdrawal of any accumulated balance from the specified instruments such as PPF may not be subject to tax. Now, senior citizens should not rush out and withdraw their money in a hurry to save tax because wherever they invest next, the interest will be taxed. Let the proposed code is introduced first. The money in a PPF should be kept there itself, if possible, as the interest earned are exempt from tax. Whenever an emergent requirement occurs, only then should it be withdrawn. Of course, a rollover from one exempt fund to another will not be subject to tax. This means you can transfer funds from your PF or PPF to a NSC or NPS without attracting taxes.

This code does propose to continue with other deductions such as medical insurance premium, medical treatment or maintenance of disabled dependent, treatment for specified diseases for self and dependents, for the handicapped, interest on loans taken for higher education, rent paid for residence, donations to certain non-profit organisations and specified institutions, and tuition fees for children.

The long-term capital gains tax on equity based instruments was exempt from taxes till now. But if code is approved, it will be taxed like short-term capital gains. This will undoubtedly affect the sentiments of investors. Now a mutual fund investor will prefer to invest in dividend mode for the dividend will remain exempt from taxes.

It appears that the new Code will adversely affect the middle class in two significant ways: (1) The taxation on withdrawal of PPF and PF, and (2) The withdrawal of long term capital gains tax. The code has been released for the public's response. It will not be wise to ignore it. Posterity will blame all of us if we, the present generation, do not participate in such a reform process for the common people. No body knows what shape code will take when it is introduced. So, do not act in a hurry.

THE BEST BETS FOR TAX SAVING
DEVICES ARE ELSS & PPF

The first few months of every year is the time to look for a tax-saving device. Most employees look for the best tax saving devices during the month of February. In corporate houses, employees need to submit their tax savings options to the account department who in turn calculates the tax liabilities for the staff, workers and executives to determine the correct deduction from their income. As February approaches, I start receiving calls from the readers of our column as to what would be the best tax saving devices during this fiscal year. It is an important query and needs to be addressed carefully.

The total limit of tax exemption under section 80C is Rs. 1 lakh per annum. All employees would get the benefit of provident fund deduction from their employers. After receiving the benefit from provident fund, the remaining gap needs to be filled by subscribing to other tax-saving devices. These devices include, among others, PPF, Life insurance, ELSS, NSC certificate, ULIP, Senior Citizen's Fund, Bank Fixed Deposit and Post Office FD.

My personal preferences are Insurance and PPF. But here is a catch. Both Insurances and PPF do not really suit senior citizens. I have advised some of my senior citizen friends to subscribe to a Bank's fixed deposit or in SCSS for five years to avail the advantage of 80C benefits. Some of my friends are holding their PPFs even after expiry of the mandatory 15 year period. I advised them to leave their money, for the 80C benefit, in their PPF accounts. However, only RS. 100.000 can be kept in PPF. For senior citizens, the best bet is to keep the money in a bank's FD or SCSS for five years, in case they have no PPF account.

NSC is good but investors have to pay tax on the interest unlike PF, PPF, and ULIP. So, it became clear that persons with existing PPF accounts should use it to park their money. It would help them greatly for there would be no tax on interest and in case they needed money in an emergency, they can withdraw cash after completing the seventh year.

A few years ago, I asked a few young friends as to why they did not want to put money in ELSS? They replied that the stock market had crashed and they felt that this was not the time to buy ELSS. I explained to them that the best time to buy ELSS was now, because the market had crashed and the NAV (at which price they would be able to buy) was the lowest. Some economist friends of mine calculated the compounded annual growth returns (CAGR) of both ELSS and Fixed Income Instrument. They found that in a period of five years ELSS gave better returns compared to a Fixed Income Instrument in spite of the great financial downturn. One of my close friends subscribed to ELSS in 2003. He confirmed that he is still in profit despite the fact that share market came down to 8900 (Sensex) from 21000. Yes, his investment from 2003 is still in profit. The share market never remains dormant in the long term. The world saw the worst financial disaster in 1932 and yet survived the depression. There surely was financial mayhem in the last recession, but nothing compared to the experiences of the Great Depression. American people did not even have enough to eat. We have already emerged from the worst of the last recession.

It would be worth mentioning that returns in the last five years in ELSS are much better than a fixed income instrument. Magnum Tax Gain's return is 27.25% and Sundaram Tax Gain's return is 22.59%. HDFC Tax Saver gave 20.56% return. Whereas the highest return in fixed income instruments like a bank FD or the Senior Citizens Savings Scheme returned 9.31%. PPF and NSC gave around 8.16%. Younger employees do not need to be jittery about the volatility in the market. In my opinion, ELSS is the best tax-saving instrument for younger investors. For senior citizens, a Bank FD or SCSS would be better if no valid PPF account is available.

A TAX-FREE ANNUITY SCHEME MAY
MOTIVATE PEOPLE FOR PENSION PLANS

I am not aware of any country, except perhaps the Arab world, where the pension received by a retiree is free of income tax. Enormous tax benefits are available while contributing to a fund. But all senior citizens of western countries pay income tax when they receive their pension amount monthly or weekly. Of course, citizens of those countries receive social security, which our citizens do not receive. Perhaps to mitigate this shortcoming, the union Government is planning to make pensions free of income tax when the new tax code is introduced for Indian citizens.

Annuity and PPF are two great schemes which would usher in a great time for retired and senior citizens and tax-paying rich single women. At present there are a few guaranteed fixed income schemes like bank FD, post office monthly saving schemes and the senior citizen savings scheme in our country. The return on capital is 7.75% to 9% in all these schemes with applicable income tax deductions. If the revised tax code is implemented, both deferred and immediate annuity will not be taxed and investors might now be more inclined to invest in pension schemes. The best consequence will be that this would not only cheer up older citizens, but greatly motivate young and middle-aged people to save more and more for their future.

Till now, everyone—school teachers to senior bureaucrats—who have been receiving pension, had to pay income tax. With the new tax code and no income tax to pay, they will naturally feel happy. Young people opting for the deferred payment option will also be greatly benefited. Widows and older citizens who were not willing to save money in the pension scheme will now be interested since the immediate annuity benefit like *Jeevan Akshay* scheme of LIC is likely to get a boost. An older person of 65 years and above will be able to invest Rs. 10 lakh in the current year and start getting pension from the next at the rate of 7.5% return without tax. This means a retiree will be able to get Rs. 75,000/—annually without tax.

Any person above the age of 40 will be able to save and get a similar return and start a systematic investment plan in mutual funds from the money received as interest. If they keep this investment system till they retire at 60, they should be able to gather at least Rs. 49 lakh even if a moderate return of 10% is considered for the period of twenty years. This amount will be free of income tax as of today, but may attract capital-gains tax at the applicable rate after twenty years.

Immediate annuities have been around for the last few years in our country. But most of the people were not interested due to the heavy income-tax rate and lower annuity value. LIC has a very decent immediate annuity policy in *Jeevan Akshay*. It was one of the most successful policies till 1992. The growth of this policy along with *Jeevan Dhara* (deferred policy) was phenomenal. Both policies went by the wayside since 1993 as no tax benefit was available. With the intended tax benefits in the new Code, the *Jeevan Akshay* policy could be a marvellous policy for senior citizens. If senior citizens have some lump-sum money to spare after investing in SCSS and PPF, I would recommend our readers to invest in this product provided they are already taxpayers. The amount received from immediate annuity would be tax free in the hands of senior citizens. The rate of return annually would be 7.60% till their demise with return of capital to their nominee. This is a fantastic return after taking advantage of SCSS, Post Office Monthly Income Scheme, and PPF.

I am also sure that with such great benefits the new Pension scheme would be a great product for the younger generation. Senior citizens will not derive the best benefit from NPS for it has no immediate annuity facilities. It would be wise for senior citizens and tax-paying rich widows or single women to concentrate on a single annuity based product like *Jeevan Akshay* for a comfortable livelihood without a tax burden.

What is immediate annuity? When a person buys an immediate annuity, he pays the life insurance company a lump-sum amount up front and the insurer gives a guarantee of paying him a fixed amount at regular intervals—depending on the payment option chosen by him—as long as he lives. On his demise the principal amount is returned back to his spouse or children. The spouse may also continue to get the same amount for her lifetime. The present rate of annuity is around 7.60% per annum. Once upon a time, during the twentieth century, it was much higher. Before 2001, LIC was the sole company that issued an immediate-annuity policy. Even now there are very few companies that provide these facilities. With the new tax provisions, more and more companies will surely start single-premium immediate-annuity plans, as it is going to be a hot product among middle-aged persons, senior citizens, and tax-paying rich, single women. The great news is that though immediate-annuity plans are insurance products they do not require any medical check ups. The return is not market related, yet the rate of annuity is higher than a regular insurance product and fully assured like a bank product. What is even better than a bank FD is that there are no tax obligations. So, get prepared and start investing in a great product for your lifetime. Do it soon because the tax benefits can be withdrawn as it was done in 1992. However, once you invest during the currency of the scheme, you will continue to get the promised benefits for life.

SINGLE PARENTS NEED A PRUDENT FINANCIAL PLAN

In our society, numbers of single parents have increased. Perhaps about fifty years ago, the number of single parents in the affluent society of Assam could be handpicked. Today, it would be difficult to count these numbers easily. Besides accidents and health hazards, the numbers of single parents have multiplied with new social problems in a changing social structure. One of my teacher-friends, Ananya Goswami, once told me that it was never easy to be single with children. She had two sons. Ananya had a happy family. Suddenly, her husband died of cancer leaving behind the family to be looked after by her alone. Ananya was only 30 years old when her husband passed away. Fortunately, she was educated and had a decent job. She had to manage all the responsibilities for the kids that were expected of both a father and a mother. Whether both parents are there or not, kids have to be looked after, brought up with love and affection, and all needs have to be met—economically and psychologically! "It was a tough call, but I survived," Ananya thankfully recalls.

SUPPORT FROM FAMILY: The situation can be even more harrowing for those who do not have supportive in-laws to fall back on and adequate financial resources in the family to withstand the catastrophe! There are instances when the mother is not qualified enough to get a well-paying job. One of my friends, Parimal, once asked me what I meant by single parent. A single parent would be a father or a mother having children without a spouse. Their spouses might be divorced or deceased. Nowadays, there are also single parents by choice. For example, film actor Sushmita Sen adopted two daughters in her prime. There are no difficulties for affluent parents to take care of his/her kids. So, here we will only discuss the plight of the middleclass family who needs a financial—and psychological-support base.

LEARN TO BUDGET EXPENSES: My most important suggestion would be that after marriage, the girl must try to understand the details of the family finances. It should not be left only to the husband to handle the finances of the family. The budget of the family, however small, should be drawn up by both the parents. This is a requirement in spite of the fact that only the husband might be the bread earner. The budget must be prepared meticulously, depending on the earnings of the family, not on the basis of the perceived requirements of the family. All young couples must adhere to the dictum "cut your coat according to your cloth." If possible, banking should be the responsibility of the wife. That would give them excellent exposure to become finance-savvy.

SEVEN COMMANDMENTS FOR SINGLE PARENTS: In case of an unfortunate event, a single parent's first responsibility would be to know her financial worth. It would be prudent to draw up a list of assets, investments, loans, and other savings and liabilities, if any. It would be wise for a single parent to retire high cost loans like credit card payments and personal bank loans. Any real-estate assets must be protected at this time. Bank accounts must be transferred to the name of the single parent only and nominees should be earmarked.

The second most important act of a single parent would be to balance the existing asset allocations keeping in mind the time horizon and risk-return profile. Investments must be done judiciously without taking unnecessary risk. Third: A term insurance for protection and security of the family is a must. If you don't have resources don't go for ULIP. You can subscribe to term insurance instead of endowment. Fourth: Invest in a bank fixed deposit first. Open a PPF account if you do not have one. This will take care of your daughter when it is time for her marriage or when your son sets out for an MBA.

Fifth: If your income permits, do invest in a diversified balanced fund under SIP for your days of retirement. Sixth: Single parents must have health and accident insurance for the security of their children. Seventh: For a single parent, a will is a must. The will can be revised as time progresses and situations changes. An executor will be required to ensure your estate is invested for proper upbringing of your children. Plan judiciously and you will live happily.

EXCHANGED TRADED FUNDS ARE FAST GAINING POPULARITY IN INDIA

Exchange Traded Funds (ETFs) have quickly become one of the most popular ways for Americans to reach their financial goals. While they've existed in some form or another since 1993, lately, ETFs have been given a great deal of attention in both Wall Street and Main Street.

So what do ETFs offer that other investment vehicles don't?

ETFs are unique in many ways and present a variety of benefits compared to other traditional investment vehicles. With that innovation and uniqueness comes a new type of disadvantage as well. ETFs are basically a group of securities that track highly recognized indexes. They are similar to *indexed mutual funds* in that they offer shares in a professionally managed diversified portfolio of stocks or bonds. What sets them apart from mutual funds is that ETFs are traded much like stocks. Rather than transactions occurring at the close of the market, ETFs are traded all day long. Their price is determined by supply and demand in the market.

Two of the biggest pluses that ETFs offer are diversification and variety. ETFs offer you a way to keep your investments diversified across a broad range of markets and asset classes. From ETFs that mirror the major indexes, to certain sectors, niche markets, and even specific countries, ETFs allow you to select an area or industry you may be interested in investing, and saves you the hassle of purchasing stocks individually. ETFs also make it easier to allocate assets into select groups. Specialized ETFs exist that can be used to support allocation targets for stock and bond mix in their portfolios, easily making diversification one of the biggest pluses to investing in

ETFs. *Diversification* can be thought of as spreading your investment rupees into various asset classes to add balance to your portfolio. Although it doesn't guarantee a profit, it may be able to reduce the volatility of your portfolio.

While they aren't the best idea for someone who regularly invests a small amount of money, ETFs may be suitable for someone with a large lump sum to invest. They tend to offer greater tax benefits than most mutual funds. Market trades have no effect on an ETF itself as no cash enters or exits the fund. Taxes are still paid at the point of sale of all underlying securities at the investor's cost basis, but not the fund's cost basis or at the expense of other invested individuals. ETFs occasionally distribute capital gains and dividends, but usually less often than other investments which means less tax consequences for the investor. Of course, ETFs do involve certain risks that should be carefully considered before investing. These risks include but are not limited to: market risk, sector risk, as well as global and economic developments. One should also consider the trading expenses associated with investing in ETFs.

As ETFs grow in popularity, so will the types of funds offered. No investment is perfect, but ETFs offer a broad range of benefits. They're easy to trade, they offer diversification and depending on your situation, they might just be an attractive alternative to mutual funds and other investments. Basically, ETFs are open-ended index funds that can also be traded on the stock market.

Compared to mutual funds, there are many advantages of ETFs: One is real time pricing; secondly, long term investors are protected from short term traders. Hence, it proves to be an ideal instrument for both long-term as well as short-term investors and also it is easy to buy and sell from the exchange. One major disadvantage of an ETF is that the investor should have a demat account and a brokering account.

There are two types of advantages over index funds—one is the expense ratio which is currently lower in ETFs as compared to normal index funds. The second advantage is the distribution cost—the other index funds have to pay a commission to the broker, while ETFs do not. So, ETFs are less expensive. In addition to the above-mentioned expenses, there also exist some "hidden" costs like transaction costs. Such costs do not form a part of the expense ratio like brokerage and STT. These transaction costs are incurred by index funds but not ETFs. This is another area where ETFs score over regular index funds. ETFs do not incentivise their product, which other regular mutual funds do, hence there is no one pushing it. But, internationally what has happened is that over a period of time people have found that ETFs are ideal instruments and they have become quite popular.

Just to give you an example—if you looked at NIFTY BeES during the worst three months of the market crash a couple of years back, you would see that among all forty funds it was ranked 11th in the down market, which clearly shows that the ETFs/index funds are working.

Bloomberg reports that the $14 billion iShares MSCI Emerging market index, the largest exchange traded fund (ETF) beat those that are actively managed. Think of an exchange-traded fund as a mutual fund that trades like a stock. Just like an index fund, an ETF represents a basket of stocks that reflect an index such as the NIFTY. An ETF, however, isn't a mutual fund; it trades just like any other company on a stock exchange. Unlike a mutual fund that has its net-asset value (NAV) calculated at the end of each trading day, an ETF's price changes throughout the day, fluctuating with supply and demand.

It is important to remember that while ETFs attempt to replicate the return on indexes, there is no guarantee that they will do so exactly. By owning an ETF, you get the diversification of an index fund plus the flexibility of a stock. Because, ETFs trade like stocks, you can short-sell them, buy them on margin and purchase as little as one share. Another advantage is that the expense ratios of most ETFs are lower than that of the average mutual fund. When buying and selling ETFs, you pay your broker the same commission that you'd pay on any regular trade.

There are various ETFs available in India, such as:

NIFTY BeES: launched by Benchmark Mutual Fund in January 2002.

Junior BeES: An ETF on CNX Nifty Junior, launched by Benchmark MF in February, 2003.

SUNDER: launched by UTI in July, 2003.

Liquid BeES: launched by Benchmark Mutual Fund in July, 2003.

Bank BeES: It was launched by Benchmark Mutual Fund in May, 2004.

ETF IS THE NEW INVESTMENT INSTRUMENT IN INDIA

Arundhuti, a teacher in girl's higher secondary school, asked her friend recently, "Do you know the meaning of ETF?"

"ETF means Exchange Traded Fund," replied Babita.

"I know that it is the extended form of the abbreviation. But how does it work?"

"No fair idea," Babita admitted.

Both were teachers and they decided to visit a banker friend in Tinsukia. The next day they went to Tinsukia and met their friend in her office. Musfiqua, the banker friend explained to them that though ETF is the name of an investment fund it is not a mutual fund. ETF is listed and traded in the share market. It can also be bought directly from the share market. It costs much less compared to mutual funds. A mutual fund pulls together money from a lot of people and invests it in shares. In ETFs, individual persons buy alone and directly from the share market. Of course they need to go through a broker. The cost of buying is much less (0.25% to 0.75%) than mutual funds (around 2.25%), but they must have an account of depository service so that ETFs bought can be kept deposited there.

"If you don't have a depository account you need to open one. But if you have already one there is no problem. Your broker will buy and send the shares to be held in deposit in your account," Musfiqua added.

"Is it that simple? I buy shares and I have a depository account. I have a broker, too. So I do not need to open any account," Arundhuti said.

"No you don't have to," replied Musfiqua, "But Babita doesn't have an account so she needs to start one. She can use your broker to manage her transactions."

"That's great! I'd like to do that." Babita sounded enthusiastic. "Is there great risk in ETFs?"

"Of course there is risk. You cannot make money without risk. If you want risk-free returns, you better put your money in the post office or in a bank's term-deposit account. But inflation will eat away a large portion of your savings. My bank's interest is 8.5 to 10% and inflation is anywhere between 9-12%. Are you actually making any money?" Musfiqua sounded very convincing.

"So, what should we do?" asked Babita.

"You can take a calculated risk. In the year 2000, the SENSEX was 3800. Today, it is 15000. If you would have bought a NIFTY ETF then, you would have made an enormous amount of money by now. In 2008 the market went down. It has since recovered. ETF is the darling of young investors. Keep in mind," Musfiqua advised with authority, "Investments must be for the long term."

What are good ETFs in the country? There are Nifty BeEs, which track NIFTY. ICICI SPICE which tracks SENSEX. There is Junior BeES, Banking BeES, Gold ETF, etc. These ETF are passively administered. So there is no risk so far as the Fund-Manager's risk is concerned. Of course there will be market risk. When Sensex goes down it will loose money and when Sensex goes up it earns money. ETFs are hugely popular in USA, amongst the younger generation. In the long run an ETF is always the winner. The volatility of the share market does not affect earnings in the longer run. So whenever an ETF is bought, it should be invested in for 10 to 15 years. When should it be invested? It is almost impossible to time the investment. It is very difficult to buy at the bottom. We had the rarest of rare opportunities a few years back when the share market had collapsed. Now, wait with patience and buy when the market dips. In the meantime get ready with your trading account and depository account. Talk to your broker, Stock Holding Corporation, ICICI, and HDFC and get set for the long term. Remember, Warren Buffet said pickup shares when most people shy away!

A NEW TAX REGIME MAY GREET TAX PAYERS FROM 2014

With the introduction of Direct Tax Code a new tax regime is expected to start from 2014. Of course, with present political uncertainty it may not be announced at all now. Up till now, new tax proposals were submitted to the parliament every year at the time of presentation of the Budget. This will no longer be required, if tax code could have been introduced as planned . . . The Direct Tax Code is a valuable document of the country like the IPC or Cr.P.C. The government does not have to change it every year. It can be changed from time to time when circumstances change.

The DTC has been introduced in parliament for debate and discussion only. The Code aims at simplifying rules, improving efficiency and bringing about better compliance. It will replace the existing Tax Act of 1957 effective April 1, 2014.

DTC originally proposed to substantially raise the tax slab for individual taxpayers. While presenting the proposal in the parliament, the original proposal was revised; still it has given substantial gains to tax payers. The code stopped the differentiation between male and female taxpayers while proposing the rebate. Senior citizens have been given a minor relief of Rs. 10,000/—more, making the exemption limit of Rs. 2.50 lakh.

The new tax law proposes to increase the income tax exemption limit from Rs. 1.8 lakh to Rs. 2 lakh. It also proposes three income tax slabs—10% on Rs. 2-8 lakh annual income, 20% on Rs. 8-10 lakh and 30% on annual income upwards of Rs. 10 lakh. (At present, income between Rs. 2 lakh and Rs. 8 lakh is taxed at 10%, income for Rs. 8-10 lakh is taxed at 20%, and above Rs. 8 lakh the tax rate is 30%).

DTC has linked the short-term capital gains tax to an investor's annual income. A short-term capital gains tax of 5% would be applicable for an investor in the income group of Rs. 2-5 lakh, 10% in the Rs. 5-10 lakh bracket, and 15% for those with income over Rs. 10 lakh.

Tax-free dividends on equity mutual funds would be a thing of past. The code proposes a 5% dividend distribution tax on equity mutual funds and unit-linked insurance plans (ULIPs). At present, dividends on equity mutual funds are tax-free in the hands of investors.

The DTC also proposes a 15 per cent dividend distribution tax (DDT) on equities. However, it has excluded the dividend paid by a subsidiary company to its parent company from any tax liability. These exemptions make sense as dividend paid by a subsidiary to its parent company means the dividend stays within the group.

The most benefits that accrues from the proposal are (1) contribution of up to Rs. 1 lakh in approved funds, such as public provident funds, would get tax deduction. (The limit at present is also Rs. 100,000). To enjoy deduction on insurance, the annual premium should not exceed 5% of the sum assured. (2) Pension funds have been made tax free and (3) Long term capital gains tax would remain tax free. (4) The code proposes an additional Rs. 5000 on investment in insurance including health cover and tuition fees for children as exempt. However, DTC has maintained the status quo on securities transaction tax (STT) and long-term capital gains tax, that is, while STT stays, there would be no long-term capital gains tax on equity and equity related instruments. The original draft of DTC had proposed to do away with STT and levy long-term capital gains tax. One of the most important steps taken in the code is to exempt HRA and LTA up to a prescribed limit. Income on house property will be taxed provided it is actually rented out. Till now it is taxed on notional basis. The proposal of introducing a fair market value in place of the actual rent received has been done away with.

The threshold for payment of wealth tax has been enhanced to Rs. 1 crore from Rs. 30 lakh. The rate of wealth tax would remain one percent. This has been resented by high net-worth people.

To us the new tax code is a welcome move. However, the tax exemption limit of Rs. 2 Lakh seems to be meagre because it will be implemented only two years from now and by that time, inflation will neutralize the benefit now given.

The new code proposes a 30% corporate tax against the existing effective rate of 33.22 per cent on account of cess and surcharges. The DTC seeks to impose a minimum alternate tax (MAT) of 20 per cent of the book profit against the existing 18 per cent. The chambers are not very happy on this issue. Tough we can never have a tax code that will satisfy all, but surely the finance minister has tried to given enough reasons to cheer.

ENTER THE MARKET ON A DIP AND PROTECT YOUR INVESTMENT

During the month of March, 2008, when I recommended my readers to enter the share market and buy large cap Mutual funds under SIP a few old friends of mine called me up and told me that they did not want to invest in such a dull and depressed market. I told them that the basic principle of investment is that when market was depressed you should get in so that you will be the first person to reap the benefits when the market turns around. My friends were not convinced. They laughed at me and hung up.

However a few young readers thought what I said was sensible and they mustered enough courage to enter the market when the Sensex was around 10,500 only. Within 120 days the market turned around and those who laughed at me called me up and started asking whether they could enter the market then. The Sensex, by then, was flat at 15,500. My old friends lost the opportunity but my young readers gained handsomely. This always happens. I advised them to hold on to their money. There would be correction after some time and it would be prudent to enter the market then. They wanted to know when the correction would happen. I admitted that it was impossible to pinpoint a date but it would be soon. The correction happened, some friends entered and some did not.

The most important trait for investors is that they must have patience accompanied by their risk taking capacity. Those investors who entered the market in the month of March 2008, when the market was in shambles, made 30% profit in 6 months. My advice to them was if you are chicken-hearted then book the profit. If you are bold and brave then hold on. There will be a correction soon but that will be followed by a gradual upturn and the Sensex may go up to 17000 points by April 2010. Now, the Sensex is trending upwards of 19000. So, during every dip in the share market you should try to buy some shares or units of large-cap mutual funds. Younger persons can buy 60% equity whereas middle-aged persons should buy 40% if they have risk taking capacity for at least five years.

One thing must be kept in mind that all this is only calculated guesswork. Nobody in the world, not even Warren Buffet, can exactly predict the behaviour of the share market and consequently of the mutual funds. The advisors and experts can hopefully wish but cannot predict. So far, no science has been perfected that can forecast the behaviour of the share market. If such predictions could have been possible there would not have been a great depression in the world. During 2008, the world was engulfed in a recession despite the fact that we now have a record number of noble laureates in Economics and large numbers of financial honchos who are rich, proud, and stand to lose a lot of money if the market crashes.

The Governor of the Reserve Bank conceded during the recession that the Indian economy will revive faster than other countries of the world but it was not possible to predict a date. It is a fact that India will, sooner or later, become the growth engine of the world economy. So we need to keep patience and move ahead and invest in a determined manner. We need to ensure safety but we also must agree to take a little calculated risk for money to be generated. However, safety and prudence should be the watchword even now, though the economy has revived.

It is absolutely necessary to switch investments in order to earn better returns. Some mutual funds provide better return for a year or so and later fail to earn better returns. Once upon a time, Magnum Global Fund and Prima Fund were the darlings of investors. Today, these are tired funds. Switching of underperforming funds usually provide scope for better earnings. The investor must try to protect his investment at all times. Investors must periodically reshuffle their investments, if they want to maximize their returns. Investing money is only the first step in financial planning. The second step is even more important: protection of the invested money.

Investors should redeem their units in mutual funds as soon as they make a 30% return. The Golden Rule of investment is that do not invest all your money in the share market or in mutual funds. Any person desirous of investing money (other than in a savings bank account) should invest adhering to the formula of "100 minus their age = % in equity." So, what should be done by small investors? The small investor must buy mutual funds only through a systematic investment plan for the long term. No investment should be done in lump sum. Another important thing before investing is that you should consult a qualified investment advisor. Thirdly, investors should set an investment goal for themselves and put in place an asset allocation strategy depending on their risk-bearing capacity. You must invest in equity or an equity-linked instrument if you are young. Older persons should be more cautious while investing in equity. No investment should be done in equity after the age of seventy-five.

Is this a good time for investing? This is the million-dollar question. I feel that there could be a correction soon and our investors should not miss the opportunity to enter the market then. If some of the investors are keen now, they can enter the market through a systematic investment plan in diversified mutual funds in the opportunity and infrastructure sectors. Consult your advisor but the final decision is always yours.

CHAPTER FOUR

Some Important Clues for Investment

THE MOTHER OF ALL BULL MARKETS IS AHEAD OF US

Many investors are worried. Since 2008, it has been a long wait for them for a good return. But in five years, the market has given them mostly a negative return or very little positive return. Some of them asked me what they should do. My reply was: Have patience. The mother of all bull markets is ahead of us. Bull market is always preceded by slumps. Those who have stayed invested since 2008 would get a return of 17% to 25% and share market would clock 22,000 or even more.

Someone asked: When will that happen?

My reply was: The exact date cannot be predicted or pronounced but all indications reflect that the bull market may start from 2015 or after. The market may go down from the end of 2012 for a year or so. Therefore, younger people should enter the market through systematic investment plan from now onwards to harvest a good return by 2015-16. Senior citizens can invest in Dynamic bond funds for a year or so, and also in corporate bond opportunity fund for thirty months. The return could be as high as 10% to 13% within the specified time.

Many of our readers have also been keen to know about the best mutual funds to subscribe. They also wanted to know whether money invested should be redeemed when the market gets into recession. I have not been answering such questions for there were no reliable analyses so far. Recently Jim Cramer, the host of the show *Mad Money* and an alumnus of Harvard, revealed his research work that seemed prophetic to me. Investment in equity could be done directly in stock and through mutual funds. There are many mutual funds that have done very well for some time in India. But not too many come in this list when it comes to consistent performance. A recent study by a national business newspaper brought out results which are amazing and to a great extent reflect the spirit of Jim Cramer's research. The results seem to be reasonably true when translated to Indian mutual funds. The analysis supports our views that in the longer term, equity provides better return. In most of our articles we have written that investment in an equity mutual fund, if kept for ten years, would provide decent returns (15 to 20%) provided the mutual fund schemes are carefully selected. For investors of the Northeast, we had recommended the mutual fund route initially rather than the direct equity route of stock.

A lot of investors probably wanted to give up after the market loss of 2008. That year was the worst 12 months for stocks since the Great Depression. But Dr. Cramer would argue against throwing in the towel. Downturn or not, high-quality dividend-paying equities are still the best-performing asset class over any 20-year period. So the people who bail out would lose out.

An analysis of returns of equity mutual fund schemes, which have been in existence for over 10 years, reveal that these schemes have greatly enriched investors who stay put for a longer period. The MF industry today has about 39 diversified equity schemes that are over 10 years old and average returns by these schemes over this 10-year period is about 20.6% CAGR (compounded annual growth rate).

However top ten best performers are as under:

1. SBI Magnum Contra: It has given an annualized return of 32.80% for the last ten years (2000 to 2010). No other asset class has given higher return than this. This return is despite the fact that during 2008 there was an almost 50% erosion of value. An investment of Rs. 10,000 in the year 2000 became Rs. 1,70,857.80 in 2010.
2. Reliance Growth: It has also given an annualized return of 32%. In the last ten years Rs. 10,000/ became Rs. 1,59,990.
3. Reliance Vision: It has given a 29% return despite a very slow return during 2007. Rs 10,000/—became Rs. 1,33,674.
4. Birla Sun Life Basic Fund has given a return of 28.5% clocking Rs. 1,25,667/—in the last decade from an investment of Rs. 10,000 in the year 2000.
5. HDFC Equity has given a return of 28.3% return. Rs. 10,000/—brought in Rs. 1,21,044 between 2000-2010.

Besides the above five funds, five other high performers have been HDFC top 200, Franklin India Prima, Templeton India Growth, Franklin India Blue Chip and Franklin India Prima Plus All of them gave excellent returns of above 24%. However, it should be noted that in the mutual Fund Industry, there is no guarantee that past performance would always be achieved. But long-term sustainability proves that those funds can be relied upon. All the above funds were five star funds from time to time. Some of them fell from the grace occasionally but recovered later. Franklin India Blue Chip is one such fund that dominated the mutual fund sector for a long time and eclipsed for a while before returning back to fame.

Besides the above funds, there are a few other funds that are shaping up well. Funds like IDFC Premier Equity, DSP Black Rock equity fund etc opened their doors recently but remained consistent players. It would be prudent for investors to check up the list of value research before starting an investment. One thing must be kept in mind that equity investment is not meant for risk-adverse people. It is rather meant for bold and patient persons. Speculation is the greatest evil in the field of money market. Patience is a great virtue if someone wants to make money. Recently Dr. Cramer of Mad Money revealed that market down turn should be faced boldly for it is the recession that provides big money in future.

Our advice to our young readers is to listen to the advice of Dr. Cramer. The risk-adverse senior citizen can avoid equity after reaching the age of 70 and devote time in debt instruments. Here is the advice of Dr. Cramer to his beloved investors. Read carefully and follow his ethics of investment.

According to Jim, "Stocks are an investor's best shot at upside, and there's plenty of academic research to prove it. These market corrections—or at times, crashes—though, are a part of the package. If you want to enjoy the profits, then you have to steel yourself to the inevitable losses. After all, there are only two kinds of investors: those who have lost money, and those who will! So, you should expect corrections rather than fear them. That's rule number one if you want to stay in the game. There will come a day when your portfolio's forward motion will come to a sudden halt. That's no excuse to quit. If anything, you'll get the chance to buy great companies at lower prices, setting up the chance for even greater gains when the market turns back up." This is Dr. Cramer's advice to young American investors. Yes, we feel Dr. Cramer's advice is prophetic for our investors too.

MARKET VOLATILITY ENSURES BETTER RETURNS

Usually, after election results are announced, the share market goes up. It is possible that the market may come down again. But that should not deter investors from buying equity. For the long run, equity is the king and as the market goes down, it is time to invest through a systematic investment plan (SIP) in mutual funds.

According to an expert, volatility is the friend of astute investors. It is actually volatility that makes you rich. A prolonged bear phase is not welcomed by new and uninformed investors. But astute investors always welcome volatility and a bear phase in the share market. According to Warren Buffet, equity is the king in the long run. This is because in the long term, the share market is bound to have fluctuations and volatility. Volatility ensures a better return if invested with prudence. If investors adhere to a systematic investment plan and a systematic transfer plan, he or she is sure to benefit. This is the point which most casual investors always ignore. For example, if the index would have remained static at 5900 (from 2000 to 2004) no one would have been able to make money. Since the Sensex went down from 5900 to 2800 (in 2002) and then climbed up to 5900 (in 2004), astute investors made lots of money. When the market went down in 2002, people who continued to follow the SIP route and kept on buying units at a lower cost reaped a greater benefit. As the market rebounded, the investors were benefited because their cost of acquisition was much lower during the bear phase. So, to be honest, the bear phase should not always be looked down at. Investors of mutual funds must keep in mind certain important points which are enlisted below.

1. Investors should not try to always time the market. Investment can be made steadily. The only point to be kept in mind is to buy in a phased manner.
2. All the money at the disposal of investors should not be invested in equity. Depending on the age and income of an investor, it should be invested proportionately in debt and equity.
3. The money required for day-to-day expenses should be invested in debt funds and a bank fixed deposit.

4. The balance of investment in debt and equity should be changed as the years pass. As investors advance in age, more money should be allocated in fixed income and less should be earmarked in equity.

5. While the share market is recovering, never invest a lump sum at one go. It should be through SIP or STP. My personal preference is STP. You can invest in a lump sum only when you are sure the bottom has been touched already. (This is very difficult to predict). Can you really predict the bottom? So avoid putting in all the money together.

Dhirendra Kumar, a well known mutual fund expert recently said, "Any investor who has followed this time-honoured prudent advice should be sitting pretty today, largely unaffected by the turmoil of 2008." He felt that the market value of your investment may be down today but since you do not need any of it for the years to come, it doesn't really matter. Long before you will need the money it will have ample opportunity to grow again. (Personal Finance, The Telegraph, 3rd Nov).

The loss during a recession is actually a notional loss. This will be made good when the market takes a turn for the good. But where is the guarantee that market is going to rebound? In the share market, nobody can predict the behaviour of the market. There was no guarantee that market would touch the bottom. Similarly there is no guarantee that market will surely move up. But our experience reveals that the market is going to go up sooner or later as there will be growth in the economy in the long term. If the world can recover from the Great Depression in 1927 there is no reason why the turmoil of 2008 cannot be handled. No doubt, these times are challenging. Depression can be seen all around. But the efforts of all the authorities to give a push for the growth of the economy are also genuine.

I would like to quote the remark of Dhirendra Kumar, "Despite the crashes, equity is a far safer option over the long run. The real danger to your financial well being is not the market crash, but the insidious effect of inflation." Yes, equity is not unsafe, what is really unsafe is our mentality and fear psychosis.

A PERIODIC SWITCH ENSURES PROTECTION OF INVESTMENT

The Governor of the Reserve Bank conceded recently that the Indian economy will revive faster than other countries of the world but it was not possible to predict a date. It is a fact that India would be the growth engine of the world economy sooner or later. So we need to keep patience and move ahead to make determined investments. We need to ensure safety, but at the same time, agree to take a little calculated risk to make money for the future. However, safety and prudence should be the watchword as the economy takes time to revive.

It is absolutely necessary to switch investments in order to earn better returns. Some mutual funds provide better returns for a year or so and later fail to earn good returns. Once, Magnum Global Fund and Prima Fund were investor's darlings. Today, these are tired funds. Switching of funds usually provide a better scope for earning. Here is an interesting conversation between an investor and an advisor immediately following the crash of 2008:

Investor: I invested a lakh of rupees in July 2006 in SBI Magnum. Today I find that my invested amount has shrunk to Rs. 60,000/-. Where do I go from here?

Agent: Perhaps you forgot to take out the money when your investment reached Rs. 1,60,000 in the month of October/November in 2006 itself.

Investor: Why should I withdraw the money in five months time?

Agent: Because you had already reached a 60% profit margin in the five month period. Even if you had withdrawn the amount after a year, i.e. in 2007, you would have made a very decent profit of 55%.

Investor: But didn't you tell me to invest for a longer period of five/six years?

Agent: Yes, I did. Let 2011 arrive and you will find a different result.

The agent smiled and left.

Nowadays, this is a typical discussion between an agent and an investor. The investor must try to protect his investment all the time. They must reshuffle their investment from time to time if they want to maximize returns. Investing money is only the first step in financial planning. The second step is *protection of the invested money* and that is the most important step of all. Investors must redeem their units in mutual funds as soon as they make a 30% return.

The Golden Rule of investing is not to invest all your money in the share market or in mutual funds. Any person desirous of investing money (other than in saving bank accounts) should invest adhering to the formula of "100—age = % in equity." Following this formula a thirty year young person can invest, out of his investment corpus about 70% money in equity. But a 55 year old person should invest only 45% in equity. A forty year old person, who has Rs. 1 lakh for investment, as per asset allocation strategy, should invest Rs. 60,000 in equity and 40,000 in bank FD or PPF or any debt fund. The debt fund will fetch 8% return whereas equity may go up by 30% in the next six years. This increase would make the value of equity investment Rs. 90,000 as against a value of fixed return of Rs. 41,600. In such a case, investors need to continuously switch funds from equity to fixed income to protect their earned income. Investments should be avoided when market is up continuously. Profits of equity should be switched over to

FD or to PPF to maintain the correct ratio of investment. Always invest through SIP to continuously keep on buying units at a cheaper cost.

So what should be done by small investors? The small investor must buy mutual funds only through a Systematic Investment Plan for the long term. No investment should be done in lump sum. Another important thing to remember before investing is that you should consult a qualified investment advisor. Thirdly, the investor should set a personal investment goal and put in place an asset allocation strategy depending on the risk bearing capacity. You must invest in equity or equity-linked instruments if you are young. Older persons should be more cautious while investing in equity. No investment needs to be done in equity after 75.

THE GREAT DILEMMA OF INVESTORS TODAY

A Los Angles based Indian, Karthik Rajaram, who was considered a financial wizard, was found dead with his wife, sons and mother-in-law in his posh house in September, 2010. He killed himself and his family members as his fortune was wiped out by the meltdown in the US. Forty-five year old Rajaram once made over 1.2 million dollars in a single deal in London. An MBA of UCLA, he was named by The Telegraph of London as the most astute investor. LA land records revealed that he even profited three times from the sale of his house before the collapse of the real estate market. Then, what went wrong? He overplayed his investment in the month of September. His entire money perished. So, my advice to my readers is never overinvest. The foremost thing to consider is the safety of your money. Invest only a smaller part of your money in share market instruments or in private sector's FD at present.

During his visit to France, the Indian Prime Minister Dr. Man Mohan Singh explained that the Indian market is now open to the world. So, it is not possible to insulate the country's economy from the influence of other economies of the world. This apprehension of the Indian Prime Minister has also started showing up in the minds of some of the investors in the country. Ranjan Das, one of our esteemed readers, sent me a mail during the severe recession a couple of years ago stating that he was in the midst of a dilemma. "What is the problem?" I asked. He replied that he was not being able to decide whether he should buy individual shares of companies or index-based investment when the country is reeling under a fiscal crisis.

I assured him that he was not a loner facing that dilemma. There are hundreds of investors who are facing the same problem. Many investors have burnt their fingers during the month of January when they bought very good shares like SBI, L&T, and Reliance, yet lost money heavily. I can only assure my readers that those shares are golden shares and no one will turn out to be a loser in the long term. But do not expect a miracle. It will take time. In share, market patience is the greatest virtue. Invest systematically for the long term only. You will find your dilemma taking a back seat, nay, vanish quickly. Now let us discuss whether buying Nifty index is better or buying individual stock is a better move.

To answer this question it will be necessary for us to address two important questions. The first one is whether individual stock is the flavour of the day or buying index is more prudent. The second question is should anyone time the market? The answers to those questions are complex. It cannot be explained in one line answers. It deserves a detailed explanation. If an investor has time and energy to do research and methodically study the share market it would be really nice to take a good look at individual stock. An index-based investment is the sum total of all the index-based shares. Only those investors who do not have time or interest for a detailed study need to buy a Nifty-Based Index Fund. When the market goes up you will be really making money, but when the market pushes itself down you will surely lose money. Now the second question arises, should we invest in Nifty index now? According to me, timing the market is an absolute taboo. Yet an investor can invest now provided he is capable of withstanding the risk if the market goes down further. It is essential to note that the market might go down even now. But it would be a temporary down turn. The market will surely come up sometime in the year 2010-11 or later. But it must be kept in mind that the share market is not for all people as lots of formalities such as opening demat account, bank account, pan-card formalities, etc. are involved in the process. So my sincere advice would be that only bold and risk taking investors, capable of maintaining the basic formalities of the investment, should enter the market. The safety of your investment must always be your top priority. Greed must not be allowed to take over the needs.

INFLATION MAY TURN INTO DEFLATION
IF NOT HANDLED CAREFULLY

Till the end of 2008, India faced the problem of rising prices. Inflation created havoc. It went out of control and both RBI, through monetary policy, and the Government of India, through fiscal measures were busy controlling inflation. The rising prices of crude oil brought in inflation and it was not possible to control the inflationary pressure for a while. But fortunately, from the beginning of the New Year the effect of measures taken by RBI could be seen and slowly the prices started falling. All heaved a sigh or relief when the first sign of falling inflation was noticed. But alas! Inflation fell rather rapidly.

The rate of inflation on 7th June 2008 was 11.66% which is almost 12%. The end of January saw inflation coming down to 3.2%. At this point of time people in general and economists in particular were very happy. Even the Government felt relieved. But come last week of February, the smile turned into a grin. The inflation came down to 2.43%. This was one of the lowest levels of inflation. Economist was not sure whether it is a good sign or a signal of incoming turmoil. People were confused to see that prices of consumer goods have taken an upward trend. What is this? Price of potatoes and onions went up by 20% in the month of March yet the official figure of inflation has gone down. In fact inflation went down by 7th of March to 0.44%. Never, in the history of modern India, inflation has gone up to this extent. By this time, some of the economists started wondering whether the country was actually passing through a state of *deflation*.

Monte Singh Alluhwalia stoutly defended that lower inflation does not necessarily mean a state of deflation. He felt that economy might register lower inflation some time but out of such a trend of inflation, the economy would rejuvenate by creating fresh demand. Though, on a few earlier occasions we did not agree with the views expressed by him on the rate of growth of the economy, yet this time we tended to agree with what he said. Yes, lower inflation does not necessarily mean a state of deflation. What is the meaning of Deflation? In common usage, deflation is generally considered to be "falling prices" while Inflation is "rising prices". Actually this is "price inflation" as opposed to "monetary inflation".

However, every month some prices are rising while others are falling. So the inflation rate is a compilation of all of these factors. Currently, we have some major inflationary forces combined with some deflationary forces. On the inflationary side we have rampant money creation, and rupee devaluation compared to other currencies. This is causing prices for food and energy to skyrocket. On the deflationary side, we have the sub-prime fiasco which is reducing liquidity for banks and causing housing prices to fall.

So there you have it, rising food and energy prices and falling housing prices . . . inflation and deflation at the same time. Many economists feel that sooner or later the rate of inflation may come down to zero. But do not panic. Zero inflation does not mean disaster. Countries like Austria and Switzerland have zero inflation but these are the countries where prices are very stable. One thing must be kept in mind—though the rate of inflation had reached 0.44%, yet the real rate of inflation compared to previous years was still higher, which does not get reflected in the maze of statistics. According to us, the prices will stabilise sooner or later. However, inflation affects the middle class harder because the prices of things they buy go up while their income stays the same. Generally, the Government walks a tightrope as it cannot inflate all its debt away quickly without destroying the economy. It faces a constant balancing act.

I am not afraid of deflation as such. It all balances out soon. What I am more worried about is stagflation. The simple definition of *Stagflation* is a "stagnant economy coupled with price inflation". This will be dangerous for our economy.

TRACK YOUR INVESTMENT PERIODICALLY

The investment of money in any asset class is not the end of a story. Your job is half done once you invest in shares and mutual funds. You must track your investment periodically. Why? All shares and mutual funds do not give you the best returns all the time. Sometime returns are poor and sometime it is very good. You need to check up from time to time as to how your assets are performing. Are your assets giving you good returns? It is not always possible to provide you with great returns. What should investors look for then? Should investor look for the best funds only? No, not really! Investors should aim for consistent returns. The returns must be risk adjusted. The Blue chip fund of

Franklin Templeton was one of the best funds once upon a time. It was a five star fund for long years. It remained one of the best funds till 2005. But suddenly it fell from grace and today it is considered as a three star fund. So what should investors do?

Investors should periodically track the performance of their investments. It is not necessary to track investment regularly. Bank Fixed deposits and small saving funds do not need tracking. Their returns are fixed for all the time. Sometimes, depending on RBI's Bank rate and Cash Reserve Ratio, the rate of fixed deposit will change. But with value of rupees going down hill coupled with higher inflation has crated panic in share market. How do investors overcome this situation? You can make money even now by buying shares of Medicine companies and companies who export their most products abroad in dollar like TCS.Till early 2007 most of the Banks used to pay interest of around 10%. Today interest rate is as low as 8 to 9% for a term deposit of four to five years. But change in rates of interest is rare. Generally term deposits are mostly stable. Once you make an investment in PPF (one of the best investment options in small savings) and MIS of post office, you can rest assured. No one needs to track these investments. But you need to keep it in mind that most of the time returns of these instruments cannot beat the rate of inflation. So your investment becomes a losing proposition as your real income goes down. However, due to the double benefit of income tax under section 80c and 10 in PPF, your investments do provide a decent return without tension. Now, some of my readers ask—in which asset class should they invest and how regularly?

Investment is a personal choice. Depending on the (a) availability of funds, (b) capacity to take risk and (c) age of the investor, fund should be deployed for investment. In one of our earlier articles it was advised that all the eggs should not be kept in one basket. Younger investors (till 40 years) can invest 60% of their investment worthy fund in an equity fund and the balance money can be saved in Small savings and

Bank deposit. The investment should be diversified into (1) Bank's term deposits, (2) small savings instruments, (3) mutual funds (equity linked & income fund) and (4) in shares. The greatest investment of course is building a place to live.

There is no age specification for starting an account of savings and investments. Nowadays, banks perhaps allow a person to open an account from seven years of age. Minors can also invest in a mutual fund under care of their guardians. Investing however is not child's play. Investors must study well, be aware of risks, and must have patience to earn well. Investment should be for the long term, if someone wants to have decent returns. If possible, investors should start investing as soon as they start earning money either through salary, business, inheritance, or gift.

One of my executive friends had a deposit of Rs. 2 lacs when he started his career. He told me that the money was saved over a period of 22 years by his uncle which was actually a gift he had received as a child during various occasions like Durga Puja, Bihu, or on his birthday. There was no mutual fund in 1964 when he joined the service. He bought shares of Hindustan Lever with this amount and later in 1991, could send both his children to study in MIT & Princeton in USA by selling these shares. A reader asked me how to judge the best picks from the mutual funds arena. You have to study books and magazines and visit web pages of mutual fund trackers. My advice is to visit www.valueresearchonline.com to find out the best funds of the last three years. But please bear in mind that today's best performer may not always remain the best fund. Past performance is indicative but not essentially always the best. Look for a consistent performer.

DO I INVEST NOW OR WAIT FOR NIFTY TO GO UP?

I must admit that this is a good question. Most of the common investors always try to invest their hard earned money when Sensex or Nifty goes up. A very large number of investors bought mutual fund when Sensex moved up from 18,000 to 21000 points. When the Sensex touched 10,750, there were hardly any retail investors to buy funds. Is it a good trend?

It is not a correct practice to time the market. No one has benefited greatly by such an act. Timing the market is a difficult proposition. Rather investors should invest their money in a disciplined way. A Systematic Investment Plan is highly recommended for any retail investor. Many people have asked what they should do now or when a financial storm is lashing the market and economy. Should we keep our money in FMP or should we use FD of a Bank only? Should we totally avoid the stock market? These are some of the questions often asked.

I have thought over the matter again and again and I feel that our approach should be:

1. We should first calculate how much money we have for investment. Once we arrive at a figure, we should find out what is our age. If our age is fifty, then we must deduct our age from a heavenly figure of 100. In this case, the result would be fifty. Now, this figure of fifty should be considered as a percentage (%) that could be saved or invested in equity. Now we need to calculate out of this fifty percent how much we have already invested in equity through shares or through mutual funds. In case we have already invested forty percent, then there is 10% left for fresh investment at present. In case you are risk averse then invest this 10% in a fixed deposit bank account. If you can withstand some risk, this 10% can be invested under

the systematic investment plan for a period of three years. It is expected that the storm lashing the financial world would calm down at some time. You would thereafter make a handsome gain.

2. "Should we avoid investment in equity?" asked a reader of my blog. My reply was he can, in case he is risk averse. But then, he should not expect to make money later. It will take time to get better return out of his already invested money since he had invested when Sensex had reached 21000 points.

3. "My investment has lost 50% value. Should we take out our money now?" asked another reader. My reply was: It is a wrong perception of yours. You have not lost money. At present your loss is a notional loss. Perhaps you may lose further notionally. As soon as you take out money, the loss will be a real loss. Can you really afford it? Have patience. Do not act in a hurry. What goes up comes down. And what goes down will come up, especially when it is the stock market. It will only take time. In 1932 the stock market crashed. The Great Depression followed. But it came up! The year 1945 saw a great rejuvenation in the USA. The Americans have not looked back. Germany faced their worst financial situation after the World War, but by the sixties both Japan and Germany became two of the richest nations in the world. We should not forget that destruction can be followed by rejuvenations. We must not panic now!

4. "I want to book my losses once Sensex reaches 15000 points to avail the tax benefit some time before the year ends. I will put the money in a liquid fund and invest through STP in mutual funds. If Sensex goes down thereafter, I will buy units at a lower cost. Can I not do that? Would that not be profitable for me?" Yes, that would be. But are you sure that the Sensex would go down just after you book your profits or losses? What happens if Sensex goes up instead? Nobody can predict the behaviour of the market. Not even Warren Buffet. We should be an investor and not a juggler! If you can predict

that Sensex will further go down after you book your profits, then surely go ahead and do as you wish. But as a matter of practice I do not recommend such a thing. If you have extra money and if you are capable of taking risk go ahead and invest systematically for the long term and make money in the right way. Congratulations to you.

INVESTORS' EDUCATION AND TRANSPARENCY HELPS IN WEALTH CREATION

Nowadays, many people approach the share market, mutual funds, and insurance with a vengeance. But most of them do not take informed decisions consciously. They try to invest because their friends and neighbours have made money in the share market overnight. This misconception of making money overnight is only a myth. In reality, many people who have not made a long term investment have lost their money. According to a good old saying, keeping all the eggs in the same basket should be avoided. The same principle is applicable in respect of investment. The earned income of persons should be kept invested in different class of investment instruments. We always need to remember that diversification is the name of the game when it comes to investment. It is the responsibility of the Mutual Fund Association and insurance fraternity to educate investors so that investors can take informed decisions when it comes to investment and insurance. Just putting money recklessly by investors in FD, Mutual fund, Stock or Gold will not help them in getting the best overall returns. While all the investors need exposure to equities to get the growth in capital and in beating inflation in the long run, debt instruments must be subscribed to avoid turmoil of the market. Hence it is advisable to invest into both equities and debt. It will help investors in getting higher returns from equities, while enjoying the capital safety offered by FD. To make investment and insurance investors friendly and savvy, the Association of Mutual fund and Insurance must play a proactive role.

In order to educate investors, IRDA has recently started clarifying important points through the media. According to A circular, partial withdrawal can be made only after five years of buying them, effective July 2010. Till now policy holders were in a position to redeem part of their investment in three years. Many investors did withdraw early which resulted in incurring heavy losses. IRDA's new rule would prevent the situation. Hopefully when people redeem after five years, there would be higher returns. The distributors and brokers misguide or conceal information at times and that damages the cause of investment rather than promoting the creation of wealth. Transparent dealing is essential to build up confidence of the clients. While vending ULIPs some distributors failed to inform the clients that premature withdrawal (at least before five years) would land them in a state of loss. But in case the full term could be survived it would give them handsome returns. Insurance companies have not given proper attention to educate the clients in this regards. IRDA has taken up the cause of protecting the insurance plans but have not taken up insurance education programme for the clients. Insurance is a product of solicitation. While soliciting business, the companies, distributors, and advisers should be truthful and transparent. The new guidelines for Mutual Fund distributors are on the anvil, according to SEBI Chairman.

With the stock market in a continuous downward spiral, it comes as no surprise that nobody wants to invest in equity markets during a recession. AMFI has a responsibility to educate their investors. The crash in the share prices during 2008 has proved to be a boon for the banks, whose fixed deposits (FDs) were ignored by the investors in favour of equities for higher returns. These banks came out with various FDs, offering attractive rates. This tempted many investors to opt for FDs. However every investor in FD must remember that FD is also an investment option and like any other investment option, it has its own pros and cons. So be prepared to get the complete overview of this investment option before choosing it. At present gilt funds are doing very well. But how many MF advisers have asked their clients to invest in a government-guaranteed gilt fund? Presently some of the gilt funds are giving high returns (8% to 10%) besides safety. The dividend out of this income is also tax free. This is an ideal option for senior citizens and risk-averse investors, at least for a year.

FD (Fixed Deposit) is also a term deposit. It is similar to a savings account, except that your money is locked in for a certain specified period, also called a *term*. Hence the name "term deposit." However, while you cannot access your money, the bank rewards you by giving you a higher interest rate than your savings account. The recent transparent direction of IRDA on death benefit is very good. In case of ULIP and Insurance, minimum death benefit payable must be mentioned from now onward and ULIPs cannot be used to obtain loans from any sources. The death mentioned would not be mandatory for ULIP, the circular stated. From now onwards, the insurance policy would have to specify the minimum commission and provide illustration of benefits clearly.

Term deposit is a good investment option but not the best one. When inflation goes up (as is the case of 2010), the real value goes down. In 2010, when inflation was around 10%, the FD rate for three years return provided interest at the rate of 7.5%. This meant that keeping money in FD would incur a loss, for the real value would go much below the rate of inflation. Remember, under such circumstances diversification would help realising better returns. People may like to invest in GOLD ETF or may like to buy paintings by reputed artists. Just putting your money in FD will not help you get the best overall returns. You also need exposure to equities to get the growth in capital and to beat inflation in the long run. Hence it is advisable to invest into equities, debt, or in gold and art segments. To overcome such situations, a few fund houses have brought in funds which invest only 25% in equity, 35 % in Gold ETF and 40% in debt instruments. It will help investors get higher returns from equities, while enjoying the capital safety offered by Gold and FD.

While discussing about the transparency and educating investors let us make some simple observations regarding Fixed Deposits in a bank. FD has various benefits that make it an ideal investment option for those looking for capital safety. But we do not recommend fixed deposit in Private Limited Companies even if that company has been a market leader in their business. Once a great company named Carrit Moran, that enjoyed an enviable reputation of being a safe fixed deposit, got busted and many investors incurred a huge loss. FDs of banks are comparatively a lot safer than equities, as a deposit up to Rs. 1 lakh is insured by the Deposit Insurance Credit Guarantee Corporation. So in case the bank fails, your money is still secure. This makes an FD an ideal investment option for senior citizens.

Global Trust Bank got busted but the deposits did not lose any money. These facts are never highlighted either by AMFI, SEBI or by IRDA. It should be noted that unlike dividends given by the companies, the interest earned on an FD is fixed, as the rate of interest for the particular term is constant. Even if the rates increase or decrease subsequent to your opening an FD, your rate of interest will not be affected. So you are guaranteed a regular income, making it an ideal investment option for those looking for regular income.

The FD of a bank helps you secure a loan in case of need. Are you looking for a secured loan? Then you can avail a loan by offering your FD as collateral. While your FD continues to earn interest, the rate of interest for the loan will be a few notches higher than that of the FD. Hence this type of loan works out cheaper than any other type of loan, since the bank has the assurance of claiming your deposit if you fail to repay the loan. It is a proven fact that for those looking for an efficient tax saving investment option, FD is a good option. While ELSS has the shortest lock-in period of 3 years, your capital is not secured. On the other hand, PPF offers capital security. It has a lock-in period of 15 years. The tax saving FD offers the best of both worlds, as your money is locked for just 5 years while your capital is safe. One thing must be kept in mind: In bank fixed deposits, erosion of worth of capital due to inflation is possible. Inflation affects the purchasing power of money. When inflation goes up, the purchasing power of money goes down. As the interest rates of the FDs are lower than the rate of inflation, the purchasing power of money deposited does go down. As a result, you end up eroding the worth of your capital. Except for tax saving FDs, the interest earned is taxed. So you end up incurring a tax liability. You are particularly affected if you are a high income earner. In equity, you are free of income tax liabilities so far as dividend is concerned and there is no long term capital-gains tax.

Unfortunately most of the brokers of mutual funds or advisers of insurance companies have not clearly stated the advantage and disadvantage of their products. The clients get disillusioned when they do not get the expected rate of return in the short term. All ULIP advisers must inform their clients that prior to four years no great returns are possible. They can take out their money, but incur a fine which would mean loss of capital invested. Transparency and investor education will only help the cause of insurance and mutual fund companies. Let the investors take a conscious decision after getting them fully informed and educated. Our society is evolving from a middle class mentality to a pro—capitalist mentality. During this transition, transparency and investor education programmes will ultimately help the cause of the insurance and mutual fund industry more than investors themselves.

The best option for a middle class investor is to invest as per his personal goals. If you have any short term goals, i.e. goals that have to be met within 3 years—like buying a car, or going on a holiday—then

FD is your best bet. On the other hand, for long term goals like retirement planning or your child's education go for equities, mutual funds and insurance products.

INVEST THROUGH SYSTEMATIC PLAN REGULARLY

Genuine investors should not try to time the market and should stick to long term investing. What is the meaning of long term? The investment horizon should be for a period of five years. Due to the occasional higher volatility of the share market, most of the time adequate returns are not delivered in the short term. High returns are delivered in one year's time only rarely. 2009 was an exceptional year when the market delivered a very high return within a year (almost 83%). This was unusual. Now the question arises what should investors of Northeast do?

The investors of Northeast are generally new investors. It would be prudent for them to be cautious. We have advised number of times that no equity investment should be made for short term. It would be prudent for investors with low risk appetite to keep away from the market. They can keep investments in a Bank FD or at best in a short-term Debt fund. Investors with moderate risk appetite should invest in MIP and Balanced Funds for a period of five years. Only persons who can withstand volatility in the market should subscribe to shares of the stock market or subscribe to a diversified mutual fund of four and five star rating by Value research.

I must admit that investors of today are lucky that the provision of Systematic Investment Plans have been introduced by most of the Fund houses. When in 1998 Templeton introduced the SIP system, most people took it to be a market gimmick. But it proved to be a great plan. The return of investment in SIP for the same of money for the same period is much higher than a lump sum investment for the same amount for the same period. For the middle class and the lower middle class it is always difficult to make a lump sum payment. They can save slowly and steadily while they keep earning every month. Earlier, systematic investment could be carried out annually, six monthly or weekly. But of late, a few fund houses have introduced a "daily SIP" provision. This would be greatly beneficial to daily wage earners and for self-employed people like doctors, advocates, and shop-keepers who receive funds daily from their clients . . . but do not know how to account for it.

Many investors of the northeast have kept themselves away from the share market because of the higher chances of loss. They keep money in Bank FDs that hardly earns them anything. Ultimately, a low return and higher inflation of food product make them frustrated. For such people, I would like to highly recommend investing in a diversified mutual fund on a daily SIP plan. This plan was not available earlier. In such a plan it would be difficult to lose money if you keep on investing for a period of four to five years. Rather, it would provide an avenue for excellent return. Srikumar Bandyopadhyay, an investment analyst, calculated and showed that systematic monthly investment in Reliance Vision Fund gave a 32.44% return while a lump sum amount gave an annualized return of 26.14% compared to BSE Sensex's benchmark return of 13.40% for a period of 10 years. Daily SIP plan is a recent phenomenon and at present ING, BharatiAXA, IDFC and Sahara have come up with a Daily SIP. I feel that Daily SIP is a better option compared to a weekly or monthly SIP. The share market is known for its volatility but nobody knows on which days the market would fall or rise. With daily SIP, investors will gain every day when the market falls because they will buy shares cheaper. They will gain when the market ultimately market goes up. It should be clearly understood that the share market does not remain static. It travels up and down depending on the sentiment of the economy. The daily SIP is the only method through which investors gain both ways, provided they remain invested for a longer time.

One of the experts mentioned that while investing Rs. 1000/—per day, through daily SIP from 1st January 2010 till 4th February 2010, an investor gained Rs. 21,853 whereas the lump sum investment mode could have provided a return of Rs. 21,252 only. This difference would be stupendous over a period of five to ten years. Not too many fund houses are offering daily SIP. But it can be organized by on-line purchase daily by investors without any extra charge.

My advice to our young investors would be to go ahead and invest through Daily

SIP. Housewives will be able to take care of their daily investment by saving some expenses of the family. It is most ideal for doctors and advocates, to park the daily income from their clients and ensure a great return without any income tax.

———————————————

CHAPTER FIVE

Insurance, Home Loan and Gold

IMPORTANCE OF INSURANCE IN LIFE

Insurance is a product that ensures safety and security in life. But even in this twenty-first century many people of India are not conversant with the product and the importance of insurance. Many people today would be surprised to learn that the first Prime Minister of India, Jawaharlal Nehru never had any insurance in his life. When he realised the importance of insurance, he had already become too old for any insurance company to issue an insurance policy. This fact was expressed by Nehru himself when he inaugurated the endowment policy of LIC.

It is a fact that most people learn the importance of insurance when their family gets struck by tragedy. It is also a fact that most people do not understand the necessity of proper insurance coverage and the impact of inadequate insurance coverage. Many people mean well and always plan to have the insurance they need, but too many wait until it is too late. One of the principal reasons people die without proper coverage is procrastination. The reason given for not taking insurance is silly. Many people feel that they can't afford it, never had enough time to discuss the policy, or shop for the right coverage, etc. But when tragedy strikes, they panic and are filled with regret for being careless.

A friend of mine, while visiting India in search of his roots, said that "nothing is more uncertain than the timing of death and nothing is more certain than life insurance coverage." He was referring to his father's death when he was six years old. For the next 12 years, it was the story of his struggling mother who raised her two sons with the money she received from the Insurance Company. Both of them secured seats in IIT, Kharagpur. It was the money received from insurance that saved their body and soul, he added. In the high tech world we live in today, buying the right type of insurance for your family is not easy! Especially, with all the media blitzes on buying life insurance . . . announcing how easy it is to buy insurance. But it is advisable to study the plan and then take the coverage. Life insurance is not the only cover of insurance. Medical, accident, and travel cover are also important.

Most people do not understand the difference between accidental and basic life coverage and the ramifications of term versus permanent. The wrong choices now will affect you for a lifetime because all these types of coverage are based on age. The older you get the more it costs! If the policy has limited benefits you may not have the claim paid when you need it the most. Term plans are cheaper than other kinds of insurance because of their lean cost structure. In term plans only, the premium administration expenses and the mortality charges are covered. There is no savings element in the premium charged to the insured. As a result of this, if the insured were to survive the term of the plan, he gets no returns. In fact, the premiums paid towards this plan are entirely written off if no eventuality occurs during the tenure of the plan. Only in case of an eventuality, your nominee will receive the sum assured. At the same time if you are considering insurance as an investment you have to go with endowment plans or ULIPs. But here the charges will be very high because these plans will impose allocation charges, fund management charges, etc., apart from the mortality charges and administration charges.

In life insurance terminology, endowment plans are referred to as "with-profits plans." They cover the individual's life in case of an eventuality; if he survives the term he receives the maturity amount. In case of an individual's demise, his nominees receive the sum assured with accumulated profits/bonuses on investments. In case the individual survives the tenure, he receives the sum assured and accumulated profits/bonuses.

As a whole, life insurance is a powerful tool to cover your unforeseen risks that can affect your family in your absence. It also works as a saving instrument which can help you in planning for your children's education, daughter's marriage, pension, retirement benefits or for any other defined objectives.

Single-Premium Term Policies are those where you have to pay the premium in a lump sum amount. The policy will cover your life for a predefined term. This plan helps you to escape from the burden of paying the premium every year. Pay the premium once and forget. It will give you cover for a predefined term. Compared to regular premium plans the premium will be high in this plan because you are paying money only once whereas in regular premium plans you will be paying the premium every year.

Regular-Premium Term Plans offer you the option to pay the premium on a yearly basis. If you don't want to make a huge one-time payment, go for this option. You will have to pay the premium every year till the end of the insurance term. Normally, in Term Plans, if the policy holder survives the policy term nothing will be returned to him. You will lose all the money that you have paid. But in this plan you get back all the premiums you paid.

Compared to whole life insurance, term life insurance is very cheap. It is cheaper because it is designed to cover you only for a certain period of time. If you want to cover your whole life, term life insurance is not suitable for you.

Term Life Insurance is good if you want to cover your family and your home in the event of your death. If you have a home loan, you can purchase a term insurance policy for the amount of the home loan. This ensures that your family will not lose their house, in the event of your premature death. You should always prefer a *guaranteed renewable policy,* so that your coverage cannot be terminated if you have any kind of health problems in the future. If you are purchasing a guaranteed renewable policy, the company has the responsibility to renew the policy after the predetermined term even if you are suffering from some health problems.

It is very important to remember that while choosing the term insurance you should make sure that the policies are convertible, so that you can switch to other plans later if needed. If you do not have a convertible policy, even if you do not prefer your plan till the end of the term you will have to continue with the same plan. You won't have the option to switch to another plan.

INVESTMENT & INSURANCE

Dhirendra Kumar, one of the most respected financial commentators, once famously stated that insurance and investment are as different as chalk and cheese. Both are necessary to human life. Yet both have to be viewed separately. Insurance is a protective shield whereas investment is a financial instrument. Both have their unique role to play and their roles cannot be interchanged. Nowadays, however, many financial advisors try to sell ULIP as a product which combines best of both the worlds. ULIP is a good insurance product but it is not an investment product. ULIP is a costly product. While marketing and selling ULIP all details are not always explained to the buyer. Since ULIP provides a protective shield, it has to charge higher mortality and administrative charges which mutual fund products do not have to charge. As a result mutual fund products are always cheaper compared to ULIP.

In the last couple of years both SEBI (regulator for mutual funds) and IRDA (regulatory and development authority for insurance) have notified their respective departments to provide better customer support to investors and insurance clients. SEBI notified that no entry fee should be charged if the investor submits an application at the office of the fund house. In case it is submitted through banks and brokerage houses, a levy of 2.25% will be charged. This direction of SEBI has gone well with investors and many investors have now started submitting applications at the mutual fund office. But unfortunately many small towns do not have offices of mutual funds and they operate only through banks and brokerage houses.

IRDA's instruction is far reaching. It has notified that while selling any ULIP products the clients should be fully explained as to what portion of their premium would go for investment and buying insurance and what proportion would be earmarked for mortality and administrative charges. In fact, sometimes both these charges are as high as 25% of the premium paid. Sometimes some insurance companies even charge a much higher percentage. From now onwards, before taking a ULIP policy clients must demand such information and the insurance advisor would be duty bound to explain the details and even endorse it with their signature.

An important point that must be understood is that ULIP products are good but not comparable with an investment product of a mutual fund. It is always better to make an informed decision. Clients who have opted for ULIP must have noticed that for the next three to four years their policy has not provided them enough returns commensurate with the premium paid. But once the policy becomes ten years old, they will be able to get better returns. Mutual funds generally pay better returns from the end of the first year itself. In many cases, mutual funds have given fantastic returns within the first three to four years. Some of the well known mutual fund houses have given almost 300% returns within three years which is impossible for any ULIP product to deliver. ULIP is not expected to provide such high return within a short time. It is an insurance product and it has great role to play in some other areas. In case a person wants a higher return within the first three to four years, our suggestion would be to opt for a mutual fund. For a protective shield, you can take a term insurance product which is cheaper. But in case you are planning for children's higher education or for your pension requirements you may like to depend on ULIP, since those are long term plans. The most important thing is that you need to make an informed decision about your life. Please don't just buy a product that someone has pressurized you to purchase. Don't forget: *Knowledge is the root of your power.*

TERM INSURANCE IS A SECURITY NET

I have always been writing that the term insurance should never be considered as a corollary and substitute for saving and investment. It is an established fact that life insurance is not an investment but a safety and security net for life. Many people have written to me inquiring if it is enough to have a ULIP without purchasing a traditional life-insurance policy at all. This would be a wrong perception. Life insurance is much more important to a modern-day family compared to saving and investment. It should be clearly understood that life insurance is a safety belt for the family. In today's world there is danger in every step of life. In my opinion, as soon as any person starts his professional life, he should cover himself with insurance, especially if he has the liabilities of a family. In case he has no liabilities at all, he can take insurance at a later date when he begins his family life.

During this period he can start investing in a mutual fund or PPF. I would like to reiterate that ULIP is not a product of investment. It is a product of insurance coupled with an investment option. It is like a two in one system, yet is not very cost effective.

One of my colleagues, Rajib Baruah, was forced by an insurance advisor to purchase life insurance coverage during his mid-career. Rajib was married and was the proud father of a brilliant son. Rajib also toured a lot. Unfortunately, he was the victim of an ambush during one of his tours in the northeast and he succumbed to his injuries. The family was left in great agony. Fortunately, only six months before this devastating incident Rajib's friend forced him to start a life insurance cover of Rs. 10 lakh that helped his family complete the education of his brilliant son. Rajib's wife and his son both admit that without Rajib's insurance, it would have been impossible for them to keep it together during the last ten years. Rajib's son is now employed in a multinational company.

My suggestion is no one should ignore taking insurance cover during their professional life. ULIP is no doubt a good product but it is costly. Whosoever has taken ULIP must have realised by now that the return on ULIP is not very encouraging during the first three years. If it can be kept alive for fifteen years, the return on ULIP should be good depending on the market conditions. ULIP is good for planning children's higher education or to utilise the money for a daughter's marriage, but not as a part of life insurance because it is costly. Middle-class people need cost effective insurance cover for their families. I recommend that the younger investors with family responsibilities should buy coverage with Term Insurance. A decade ago, coverage for Rs. 1 crore for a 30-year old woman would have required an annual premium of about Rs. 50,000. Now some of the private life insurance companies like Birla Sun Life are offering a similar coverage for an annual premium of around Rs 15,000. Competition has made insurance cheaper now.

Term insurance is an easy and cost effective way to protect the family. Life insurance has never been as cheap as it is now. I am happy that insurance companies have realised that more and more people would be attracted to insurance provided they bring down the premium. They have done this without much advertising, so I thought it would be prudent for me to inform my readers to consider term insurance, in case they are planning to purchase insurance cover for life.

Without much publicity, life insurance companies have drastically reduced premium rates on high-value term insurance policies of Rs. 1 crore and above. I understand recently that some other life insurers, such as ICICI Prudential Life and HDFC Standard Life, have also reduced their term insurance rates. The term rates for LIC policies, too, have come down drastically as compared to 10 years ago. A few months earlier, a few readers of our column wrote to us asking for advice on term insurance. At that time, the insurance premium was not as cheap and reasonable as now. Those readers should now contact their insurance companies to reassess their requirements of term coverage.

Buying a Rs. 1 crore life insurance cover was never so cheap. There is perhaps, a quiet rate war raging among insurers that has brought down the cost of a Rs. 1 crore coverage policy to Rs. 15,000 from over Rs. 50,000 per annum a decade ago. A big chunk of the reduction has happened only very recently. While doing this, the companies have brought down the premium without much fanfare. It should be understood that Term Insurance is a cover where the benefit of insurance would be available if the insured dies during the term of the policy. It is an annual policy like motor insurance and in case the person survives, the premium is not returnable. Term Insurance is a basic product of life insurance and every company has its own range of premiums. Quotations are available from the websites of insurance companies or from their advisors. Generally, most insurance advisors do not suggest term insurance as their commission may be very low in this insurance.

Why has the premium of Term Insurance come down recently? Perhaps, many people, especially the upper-middle class now have access to quality healthcare and lead a relatively superior lifestyle and their life expectancy is higher than before. This must have translated into lower rates.

I understand from some of the insurance officials that term-insurance premium rates have started declining since the last five years. Over the last couple of years, the premium has dropped by nearly 30%. One of the reasons for this, an official explained, is the increasing demand, mainly from the high-net worth segment, which has inflated volumes. It is possible that increasing volumes are driving the rates down and lower rates, in turn, are stimulating the demand for term insurance now.

However, one thing must be kept in mind. The price reduction is limited mainly to high-value policies targeted at the middle and upper-middle class segment, i.e. people earning Rs. 30,000 and above per month—who seek policies entailing a sum assured of more than Rs. 25 lakh. But there is a strong possibility of reduction of premium for lower middle-class people also. People must be vigilant. HDFC Standard Life Insurance, for instance, has reduced the premium rates of its term plan by around 25% across different premium and age bands. This is good news for the time being. I would again reiterate that life insurance is not a product of investment. It is a safety and security belt for the family. In today's uncertain times it should not be ignored when there is a drastic cut in premium rates.

IS GUARANTEED RETURN OF INSURANCE
A GREAT PRODUCT?

Insurance is a product which ensures safety and security of persons. The importance of insurance is unparallel in its effectiveness in the time of distress. No other product can replace its worth at any time. I have always recommended that the main wage earner of the household must insure himself to protect his dependents from economic distress in case he ceases to exist suddenly. How much should be insured and when should insurance start? These two questions have been asked repeatedly by friends, relations and wage earners nowadays. No fixed amount can be recommended for life insurance. It would depend on the person who wants to take a policy to protect his dependents. It is generally dependent on his income and on his capacity to spare money for a longer time. But as a thumb rule, a person should take an insurance policy at least five times of his gross annual salary, if he can afford it. For example, if a person's gross annual income is Rs. 20,000/—then he should insure for at least Rs. 1 lakh.

Recently many insurance companies have introduced a new guaranteed-return product. The insurance companies have tried to attract and lure investors from investment products as the equity market is in doldrums. They have introduced a guaranteed return product with insurance benefit, tax benefit, and tax rebate facility under section 80c of IT act. But the companies have not really spoken out the full truth on the rate of returns. The subscribers to such a policy should be educated fully by the insurance advisors about the implications of such a product. It is, no doubt, a good product but those persons who want to purchase such a policy must make an informed decision before subscribing these insurance product.

Insurers	Compounded return (after tax)	Single premium In Rs.	Maturity benefit	Benefit on death
Religare	7.20%	50,000/-	Rs. 1,00,211	2.5 lakhs
IDBI Forties	6.85%	51,000	Rs. 1,00,000	2.57 lakhs
Aviva	7.00%	1,00,000	Rs. 1,96,715	5 lakh, first year, less later years.
LIC Jeevan Astha	7.40%	48, 975	Rs. 1,00,000	3 lakh first year 1 lakh later years

From the table above you can notice that the best return comes from *Jeevan Astha*. The return is 7.40% (without tax). No doubt from the point of view of insurance product it is a good return. It is just above the present rate of inflations of 6.80% which is expected to come down further. Yet, PPF provides still better return of 8% (without tax). The guaranteed return in the insurance product doubles up only in 10 years. The only saving grace is the insurance benefit. But in this case also the real monetary benefit would be available during the first year only. In the later years, the benefit is equivalent to the insured amount only. It will be much more appropriate to take a Termed Insurance and subscribe to PPF for better guaranteed returns.

LIC has advertised with great hype that the *Jeevan Astha* policy will provide a guaranteed return of 10%. But when you calculate, taking into account tax-free elements, the return reduces to 7.40%. This fact needs to be told to the policy holders. How good is this guaranteed return policy as an insurance product? These products are meant for the shorter duration of five years and ten years so it is not very alluring unless someone dies either in accident or of sudden illness like a heart attack or renal failure. The pre-tax benefit is higher but after deduction of taxes it comes down substantially as shown in the chart.

Among all the guaranteed insurance products, LIC's *Jeevan Astha* could be a better product. But it would always be better to take PPF with term insurance. However, the best bet would be to subscribe to ELSS for it has given a return of 14.39% even in the worst period of the last17 years. If you can face risk, take ELSS. Otherwise, go for PPF with term insurance or subscribe to a guaranteed product of insurance. The choice is yours.

AMERICAN INSURANCE FAILURE AND INDIAN ULIP

Seven out of ten readers of our column have recently asked how safe ULIPs are. Investors are worried and scared now. Why are investors scared to invest in a unit-linked insurance plan? The recent financial trouble at AIG insurance company in America has chilled the spines of most ULIP investors. But one thing must be kept in mind that ULIP is not an instrument for investment but a product of insurance linked to market return to a great extent. ULIPs are safe instruments. Some ULIPs are really very innovative. Companies like ICICI and HDFC have introduced great products. I have no hesitation to recommend investment in ULIPs provided insurance advisors explain the nuances of ULIP in detail. The ULIPs of TATA AIG are also good despite the down turn of AIG in America. My research revealed that no large-scale funds have been passed over by TATA AIG to the US and the company has maintained a decent margin as required under law. There is no reason to panic.

One of my friends subscribed to ULIP with a yearly premium of Rs. 1 lakh. He was told that he can take out money within five years. When the policy document came he found that out of Rs. 1 lakh the company had already deducted 20% as mortality and administrative charges. He was surprised to find that the company had invested only Rs. 80,000 in the units though he paid a premium of Rs. 1 lakh. He felt morose.

He also felt cheated. It was not the fault of the plan. ULIPs are usually costly. This is due to the fact that it provided for life insurance. This fact was not explained clearly to my friend by the insurance advisor. As a result, he remained dissatisfied. He noticed that his account statement was in the red for a long time. My friend became restless and withdrew the money before the fifth year. He incurred a huge loss. Had he kept it for ten years he would have been a gainer. My sincere advice is to learn the implications of such plans fully from your Insurance Advisor before investing in a ULIP. Do not invest till you are fully satisfied.

The share market at present is volatile. It has shown signs of weakness. Many people have asked whether this volatility should worry participants in equity through ULIP. ULIP is best for generating long term wealth over a short term income. It is now a proven fact that equity outperforms the other class of assets over a long term. It can give annualized return of 15 to 20% if kept for ten years and more. For any insurance product you actually need a prudent Insurance Advisor. In ULIP, the time horizon plays the most critical role. If you cannot afford to block the money for a longer term do not subscribe to ULIP. It is necessary to keep in mind that the portfolio of ULIP is managed with a long-term perspective. So the hindrance of short term swings in the market is automatically countered. In fact, ULIPs invest both in equity and debt instruments, so they can change the ratio if they wish. When the market continuously goes up for a long time, they switch a portion from equity to debt fund. Again when market crashes, they can switch from debt to equity fund. This flexibility is a unique virtue of ULIP. You don't usually have this option in a mutual fund investment. Now the market has almost reached rock bottom. This is the time you need to switch money from debt to equity for it will now be time for equity to march ahead and touch new heights.

My suggestion to existing ULIP holders is to stay invested. Do not exit before seven years. You will incur a large loss if you do. Use ULIP for retirement benefits or for your child's marriage or for funding higher education. A decent approach for an investor now would be to keep away from ULIP for the present. Take term-insurance cover now. Invest in a Fixed Maturity Plan for more than one year at 11% to 12% return. It will be prudent to strike a balance between returns and life coverage. According to a friend of mine, ULIP is like a double-edged sword. It can either protect you and or eliminate you if handled carelessly. ULIP is not bad for the long term but presently you better postpone the decision to enter.

HEALTH CARE POLICY IS A MUST FOR ALL FAMILY MEMBERS

Health insurance coverage is a must in today's society. During the fifties and sixties of the last century, the government-run civil hospitals admitted common people whenever they fell ill. Then hospitalization was inexpensive. I still remember the birth of my only son in 1967 at Gauhati Medical College, under the care of the legendary obstetrician Dr. Rajkumar Das. The cost of the entire delivery was Rs. 165/— . . . in a paying cabin. Today, the cost of childbirth in any decent hospital is astronomical. Very often, the cost of delivery nears one lakh rupees. Healthcare costs have become prohibitively expensive. Even a minor surgery has become nearly unaffordable. To protect the family and to keep tension away, any person who can afford it, should take health coverage. It is not only essential, it is a must for self-employed persons and their family members, not to mention all retired persons. Government employees and employees of well-known corporate houses of course get medical cover even after retirement. But most of the private sector organizations don't take health covers for their employees after retirements. Yet people should take medical insurance from their mid age in spite of the fact that their employers provide them with health care facilities.

Fortunately, all the employees and their families are mostly covered by their employers. But many companies and even the government do not provide medical cover for old parents of their employees. The medical expenses are generally higher during old age and as such special care should be taken by the children for their parents. Unless insurance cover is taken by the late fifties, very often insurance companies hesitate to issue cover to older persons who have crossed sixty years of age. But recently the central government has issued directives to insurance companies to issue the policy to senior citizens after a proper health check-up. Family floater policies are available. Now even daughters can take care of their parents after marriage. The Indian joint family is clearly on the health insurance policy now.

Health insurance is obtainable by both individual policy or by group policy. Generally, group policies are issued to corporations, societies, and establishments. Generally, an individual policy is costlier and a group policy is cheaper. In India both public sector insurance companies and private sector insurance companies issue health care policy. The premium of nationalized insurance companies is a little less than private sector companies. Premium paid by people get income tax deduction up to Rs 20,000/—and additional amount of tax rebate is available for the policy of their parents. In lieu of the premium, the insurance company covers the insured in case of critical sickness and accident. Till now, dental treatment is not covered. But slowly some of the insurance companies have included dental treatment in their policies, of course, with conditions. The great change in benefit is in the area of maternity care. Till now, maternity care for non-corporate was not included. But recently cover has been issued for individuals also. This is great news for non-working mothers.

Beside group and individual insurance cover, special plans are also available for elderly persons, veterans of armed forces etc. Medical insurance covers expenses of the hospitalisation, doctor's fees and medicine etc only on hospitalization of patients. No medical expenses are paid for treatment at home. But the expenses of domiciliary treatment are also available under certain conditions. The cost of treatment is generally reimbursed and under certain condition cashless options can also be availed. This policy is popularly known as "MediClaim Policy". In addition to general health care policy another policy known as "Critical Illness Cover" is also available under separate or as additional cover on payment of an additional premium. Whenever any claim is preferred under the critical illness cover scheme, a lump sum insured amount is paid besides the usual medical reimbursement, to take care of prolonged medical requirements. The policy stands terminated after such payment is released. The critical illness cover is available for heart illness, kidney treatment, cancer etc.

The health care policy is beneficial to family members of the insured in many ways. According to a specialist of insurance, the benefits under health cover are manifold. It helps in securing a better future by paying a fraction as an expenditure today which is called the premium. It provides financial security to the family members. Health plans, unlike life insurance, requires a renewal of contract every year. Till now it was a problem that some insurance companies refused to renew insurance if claims are made too often. However some new companies like Apollo Munich and Max Bupa have now schemes for lifetime renewal. The immediate premium is slightly higher but the insured can live through their old age without nightmare and trauma.

Fortunately, most employers take care of their employees. But self-employed persons like consultants, doctors, actors, lawyers, singers, and artists must take medical cover. Most self-employed people remain busy and forget to take care of their own health. Unfortunately, not so many people get health care facilities after retirement. They need to take MediClaim policy when they are on the verge of retirement at 58 years. Health coverage is not a luxury. It is a necessity of life. Let us all be prepared for good healthcare since health is the actual wealth in life.

WOULD GOLD RULE THE WORLD IN THE FUTURE?

Gold, at present, rules the monetary system of the world only indirectly. Though all countries depend on the deposit of gold in their vault to produce legal tender required by them, yet pure gold standard is almost obsolete now. The world has abandoned the gold standard in favour of the so-called "paper money," and only a diminishing group on the far right continues to call for its return. However, if mainstream economists (on both the left *and* the right) have anything to say about it, there will never be a return to "that barbaric relic," as John Maynard Keynes called gold over 60 years ago. However, many countries buy and sale gold as the situation demands. India once sold out their gold deposit to meet the monetary contingency and recently it did buy gold twice from Russia to strengthen its power to produce more legal tender. Though there are costlier commodities like diamond and platinum, yet only gold has become synonymous with power. Gold has reached this position of strength due both to its practical and psychological value. Many people also relate with Gold better than any other commodity. Gold is sought after by most nations. It is also the favourite of vast number of Indian population.

Now, the question arises whether buying gold is a better personal investment strategy as the share market is not doing well for some time now. On the contrary, gold prices have steadily gone up. Many investors have asked whether to buy gold coins or Gold ETF . . . I always recommended individual citizens that for investment purpose the buying of GOLD ETF is better than buying solid gold. At least the cost remains secure. But in case of marriage and lifestyle enhancement, it is better to buy solid gold.

Now, it is quite likely that most advisors do brief investors that gold prices never fall; it is an ultra-safe investment. The countries around the world have positioned their currencies on gold-exchange parity by printing money, therefore gold will never fall in value, and by virtue of this operation gold ETF is risk free. But, you need to be aware that these are merely opinions.

It is surely a fact that Gold prices could continue to rise, or they can drop like a stone. Investors can make money, but they can lose money as well. However, most of the time, investors will make money—of course with moderate gains. It cannot match the return of equity in long run. So, individual investors should invest only about 10% to 15% of their total investment portfolio in gold. How much profit should be expected from gold over a period of five years? My wild guess is 10% to 18%. History and statistics tell us that in ten years, equity and art form are the best investments followed by houses and gold.

There are several gold ETFs in our country. With the exception of Quantum—1 unit of every gold-ETF represents 1 gram of gold. If that's the case, then why does the price of these gold ETFs differ?

Gold ETFs own gold, debt and other liquid instruments and cash. The combined value of these assets divided by the number of units in the gold ETF constitutes the NAV of the ETF. The NAV of gold ETF can be seen on its website, so you can see that the Benchmark gold ETF GOLDBEES had a NAV of 20000 in March 2011. However, since an ETF trades in the stock exchange and there is a different price at every tick the price of the ETF can be different from its NAV. The NSE website shows that the last traded price on that day for GOLDBEES was Rs.20010/-

This means that the ETF was going at a discount of about Rs. 10 at that point. There are big market participants who are engaged in actively trading the ETF to bring the market price closer to the NAV and gain from any arbitrage opportunity available.

All ETFs have expenses that are paid out by selling gold holdings or using the income from their debt holdings. So, although theoretically one unit of gold ETF represents a gram of gold, in reality the gold holdings are slightly lower due to the expenses. The higher the expenses, the lower would be the NAV, and consequently the trading price of the ETF.

A good example of this is the Reliance gold ETF which had a NAV of 1920.20 on 13th Feb 2011, and was trading at Rs. 1913 on that date. So, expenses eat into the NAV of the various ETFs, and affect their prices.

"Which is the best gold ETF in India?"—This question keeps popping up from time to time. According to me right now the Gold BeeS ETF from Benchmark Funds has the lowest expense ratio of 1%. Quantum Funds comes second with 1.25%. All the other funds charge higher expenses. The lower the expenses—the better it is because it leaves more on the table for investors.

I found that Gold BeeS, which has the lowest expenses, also has the highest volume, and by a large margin too. If I had to invest in a Gold ETF, it would be this. In case someone does not have d'mat account, then he should buy Gold funds from HDFC, Reliance or UTI. He can also think of buying Gold Coins as well from banks. However, the bank don't buy back gold. Investors need to sale it to jewellers at a price which is lower than market cost despite its great purity.

Continued international depression has made Gold a hero presently. But a time may come when countries may not be required to depend on Gold for their monetary policies. A new commodity may take its place in future. What would be that product is not known to anyone yet. So the gold bugs would have to resolve historical and theoretical challenges of King-Midas' proportions before they could ever reinstate the gold standard. Since a workable gold standard requires a tremendous amount of design, effort, regulation and safeguards, we might as well use fiat money, which is already simple and enjoys a successful track record.

GOLD POWER CAN NOT PROVIDE UNLIMITED SECURITY

Gold is a powerful asset from time immemorial. Even the world's monetary system revolves around Gold. The Gold standard has been the key for devising the monetary system of the world. The currency of individual countries revolves around the Gold Standard. Yet, Gold is not the best asset class, though generally it is considered as a safe bet. In the last 20 years, the best asset class has been art forms and equity ranks next to it. In effect, gold is below equity next only to real estate. However, Gold ETF has occupied a position higher than equity in last three years. But we need to keep it in mind that in the long run, the position of Gold ETF would only be behind equity.

Today, the rise of gold prices seems unstoppable. They've reached levels that would have been unimaginable a few years ago and gold cheerleaders say they are on their way to levels that are unimaginable today.

When investors go and look for information on whether gold is still a good bet, there are experts who loudly proclaim that Gold is the only commodity which will save the financial crisis of the world. They recommend buying of Gold ETF or Gold ornaments so that during the financial deluge they would survive better than their neighbours. Many experts do advocate well-reasoned arguments supporting as to why the yellow metal prices would continue to move northwards. Gold is generally accepted by all. Hence, demand of Gold is unending. There is shortage of Gold in the market and demand moves up as more and more countries would like to hoard it. There are many variations to these arguments, but basically, they all bow down to the age old theory of "safe haven" viz. that investors are scared of the bleak future of stocks, bonds, currencies and all other kinds of financial investment. They are thoroughly apprehensive of the fact that there will be another financial crisis. To survive such a financial catastrophe, it would be desirable to act smart now itself and rush to acquire an asset type that has a historical reputation of creating and protecting wealth in worst times.

Nowadays it is not just the financial experts, but even the print and electronic media who carries stories and articles recommending gold as a significant chunk of an individual's investment portfolio. They have declared that the time has arrived when Gold needs to be considered as the saviour during a financial disaster. According to those experts, time has come when Gold will have to be considered as a mainstream financial investment. But we do not think so. We would like to forewarn our readers that though gold is surely a valuable metal, it cannot be considered as the saviour of life during a financial deluge. Or is it hype only? If so, will gold live up to the hype created by some of the fiscal experts? I do not think so. According to Dhirendra Kumar, an honest and sincere expert on the field, "the hype has now reached impressive levels. On the internet, it's not difficult to find apparently sane analysts who say that in five years, gold could rise to four times of what it is today." But does he believe it? I do not. I am sure Dhirendra Kumar does not believe it either.

Projections of two to three times today's price levels in a year or two are commonplace. Is this a bubble? The gold of today is not the gold of yesteryears—a largely physical asset that was a safe haven in troubled times. This has turned into a commodity and is a paper asset too, with highly liquid and highly leveraged markets where derived proxies of gold trade in much larger quantities than any underlying demand. This bubble is likely to burst as was the case of Liquid Black Gold. Crude oil also created a bubble a few years back. Over the past few years, oil, copper, nickel, wheat took its turn in creating bubbles. We think this is the turn of the yellow metal to create a bubble. We need to be aware of such a situation and try to salvage our own position before the Gold bubble bursts.

One financial expert did say, "In fact, gold is even more of a bubble because it is an inherently useless material, earning no dividends or interest. There's no industrial consumption story like copper or nickel here, and unlike oil, there isn't any danger of "peak gold" laying waste to the world economy. Gold is the purest of all bubbles—where even the story being told by its proponents is that they expect its price to rise because everyone expects it to rise". We do believe that Gold is a valuable metal. But what we do not believe is that Gold can actually act as a saviour of humanity. It has never saved humanity, not even during the great depression. So, it would not save even now. Yes we can buy Gold for our ceremonies of the future. We can at best invest in Gold only up to 10 percent of our total investing asset.

Of course the present bubble will continue, and brave persons can find this opportunity to milk yellow cow for all it is worth. Bubbles are, by definition, irrational and emotional. Due to psychological effect and trick of the traders, the price of gold might go up phenomenally within a few years. But it is not worth taking the risk unless you are either a fool or too intelligent to exit just before the bubble bursts. A few readers asked us whether it is worth taking the risk. My reply would be similar to an up country economist who said, "If you invest in it today, have no illusions that you are putting away money for a rainy day". Buying Gold more than your own needs would be actually a speculation. Buying of the yellow metal in large volume is only a madness of the market. And this madness may continue for a while. The day is not far when this madness will end suddenly, and the experts on yellow metal will have to run away never to return back to the market. Our advice to our readers is to be vigilant. Invest in Gold in moderation. It is a valuable product but it would neither make you super rich nor support you as the saviour during a financial deluge. Your portfolio should surely consist of Gold and Gold ETF but not more than 10% to 15% of your total asset.

INVEST IN HOME LOANS

There were times when the People of Assam used to construct houses at the fag end of their career. People think of possessing a house, and construct it just before their retirement days. Firstly, they choose and buy a plot of land. After a few years, they fill up the low lying areas. It was left unutilised to consolidate and there after the house was built. The construction of a house was an arduous task. It used to be a major event in a family. I still remember the film directed by late Dr. Bhabendra Nath Saikia entitled "Sarothi". How the father toiled to build up his dream house and to provide security to his family! It was a masterpiece depicting the psyche of an Assamese middle class bread-earner who tries to establish his honour by ensuring happiness and security of his family.

Gone are those days when people used to construct their own house nearer to the retirement age. Nowadays, more than the house people crave for apartments. Instead of constructing houses people tend to buy houses, flats or apartments at a much younger age. Earlier it was difficult to get loans from banks. Nowadays, banks run after the clients to persuade them to take loan. Some of our friends have asked me whether it is worthwhile to buy an accommodation early in life. My response was positive.

When should we think of building/buying a house or a flat? My answer is as early as possible. After joining a service, a person should open an account in a bank. Try to save some money from the beginning of your career. Open a PPF account in a bank or post office. Take a term insurance if there is a family to look after. Then relax for a while, allowing your savings to consolidate. Then if you feel comfortable, go ahead and search for an unencumbered asset to buy. That is the first thing to do.

Where from should property be bought? You should always buy/build assets from a reputed builder. Try to avoid smaller contractors. A few banks like ICICI and HDFC also help people to search out home accommodation. Take professional help from them. Generally, the bank provides 80% of the value of the flat as a loan. The balance 20% shall have to be provided by you. You should go ahead buying a flat or house when you are in a position to organize initial payments.

While shopping around for loan you will realize that the interest rate varies—from fixed to floating rates. If you opt for floating rates (which is lower) interest charges are subject to change later depending on prevailing bank rate. The fixed rated loan is fixed and doesn't fluctuate with the change of bank rate. But the cost of a fixed-rate loan is higher. One of the readers asked me what type of loans should be taken. It depends on your ability. When you predict that interest rate may go up in the future, it is appropriate to take fixed rated loan. When you predict that rate may go down after sometime, you can take floating rated loans. Since home loans are taken for a longer term like twenty to thirty years, it is prudent to take floating loan for the interest rate goes up and down in a longer period. While negotiating a loan try to get some bargain. Please keep in mind that home loan rates are not etched in steel bars. Bank and financers are always willing to negotiate the rates. You can get 0.5% to 1.0% discount on initially quoted rate if you can do a hard bargain. Besides you also ask for some freebies like a waiver of processing fee or free insurance for the property. So do your homework and shop around before striking a deal. Some banks ask for a guarantor. You can bargain for not having a guarantor at all!

Why have I recommended a home loan early in life? It is because you are trying to build up an asset by paying slowly. It is a secured investment. You also get huge income tax rebate for the principal amount and also for the interest amount you pay to the bank. Building up a secured asset is not an easy job. While the value of a house goes up as days pass by, the value of other assets like a car always goes down. Buying a car is an expense while buy an accommodation is an investment too. It is a huge secured investment for life! Besides, if you can acquire an asset early in life there would be less tension later. You would be able to spare time in building your own career and secure your children's education too!

CHAPTER SIX

Mutual Funds and their Impact

INVESTING THROUGH MUTUAL FUND

What is a Mutual Fund? A Mutual fund is a fund set up by investment companies known as a Fund House. The companies collect money from public and corporate bodies, for the purpose of keeping the money in trust and to invest in share market from time to time and distribute the earning through dividend and through redemption of capital by investors. What is the benefit of investing through mutual fund? (You can read a book: *Mutual Funds* by Mark Mobious.)

Mutual fund companies collect a large common pool of money and can invest in a number of companies which is impossible for an individual to do. The investment is done through an Asset Management Company under the leadership of a qualified Fund Manager. The fund Managers are experts in buying and selling of shares. The Fund Houses are supported by a pool of researchers who find out what the best shares to pick are and when to sale them. They also see whether mutual funds are risky propositions.

Yes, there will be risk involved when investment is done through mutual fund. But it is less risky compared to the share market, due to a large diversification of the product. The diversified funds are less volatile compared to sectarian and thematic funds.

How many types of mutual funds are there?

There are various types of mutual funds. There are equity based mutual funds as well as income funds known as bond funds. Bond funds are less volatile compared to equity based funds. But returns are also lower than equity.

What is the general pattern of returns of equity based mutual funds?

The returns of mutual funds cannot be predicted. There cannot be any assurance of returns from mutual funds. Yet large number of people and Corporate Houses invest through equity mutual funds. They get dividend and benefit from good capital appreciation. During the last few years highest returns from a few equity based mutual fund was 70% per annum and the lowest return was—30% for a few months. The record of the last three to five years revealed that in an average, return of good equity based mutual fund has been 22% to 51% annually. All mutual funds are not diversified. There are balanced fund too, where sixty percent funds are invested in equity and 40% funds are invested in debt. There is equity linked saving schemes (ELSS) where income tax benefits are available under section 80C. The index fund is passively managed funds and mirrors the Sensex and the Nifty usually.

What is the greatest benefit of investing in mutual fund?

The equity linked mutual funds are tax exempt. Neither dividend is taxable nor is capital appreciation taxable, if kept invested for more than one year. The dividend of income funds are also tax exempt but capital gains tax is applicable. There are liquid funds where money can be parked and returns are as low as 8%. Amongst the mutual funds, Arbitrage Funds are the least risky and can earn 8.5% to 9.5% returns. The arbitrage funds are considered as equity funds and the same tax provisions applies to them. The HNI generally keeps a large chunk of money in arbitrage funds to escape volatility and avoid income tax.

Is it essential to invest in mutual funds?

There is no compulsion to invest in mutual funds. Why do then people invest in them? The answer is simple—to make money without paying income tax and to beat inflation. If the entire money of any individual or corporate house is saved in small savings instruments, it would provide total security but may not be able to beat inflation. The present return of most of the small saving instruments is 8% to 9%. With the imposition of income tax, the real income would go further down. Since inflation is around 8%, the entire earnings would be less than the rate of inflation. So it would be prudent to selectively invest in mutual funds.

How much money needs to be invested in mutual fund?

This is the million dollar question. The amount of savings would vary from individual to individual. The capacity to save not only depends on the earning of an individual, but also on how s/he spends. As a thumb rule, a person should invest out of his savings as per the following formula: 100 minus Age = investment in equity mutual fund. If the age of a person is 40, then he can invest 60% of his savings in mutual funds. The balance amount can be saved in a debt instrument. Investment in mutual fund should be done only by people who understand risk and can invest for the long term only, meaning three to five years, through Systematic Investment Plan.

HOW TO FACE THE DEPRESSED EQUITY MARKET?

The Equity market is volatile and depressed now. The Sensex is almost at the lowest level. The market pundits are crying wolf. Many of our readers are panicky. The fear of losing wealth has brought in tension. One of our readers called me and said, his blood pressure is high. He needed help. I humorously replied to him that it was impossible for me to treat him as I have never studied Medicine and instead studied Economics. I could suggest measures to solve his economic ills only. He cried out, "For God's sake, help me out with your advice. I am really passing sleepless nights."

"Why did you invest in equity?" I inquired.

"I invested in an equity mutual fund to make instant profit. Everyone, in our neighbourhood invested and made money. I also joined them," he replied.

"For how long did you want to stay invested?"

"For nine months only. I had to send money to my son for his last semester on the tenth month," he replied. He did not gain anything and rather lost even his capital.

My sincere advice to all my readers is that never invest for the short term in equity. It is dangerous. Why lose sleep when you can stay happy investing for long term? Short-term investments can be made only in a bank or in short-term liquid funds. Never ever invest any money in buying shares or in equity funds for the short term. Invest that much which you do not need immediately and can spare for long time.

The share market is not for those who are chicken-hearted. Be bold and be patient and you can be the winner. My friend A. R. Basu,

Finance Director of a multinational company said that he had invested Rs. 22 lacs on maturity from RBI Bond in the first week of January. The market crashed during the last week of January. It further went down in June and now his 22 lakh has become Rs. 10 lakh only. He is still smiling, working hard and waiting for a recovery. Why is he cool? For, he has no fear. He has not panicked. Why? He knows that market is going to recover sooner or later. He has invested money for a long term, at least for a period of five years. Another financial wizard, D. K. Duttagupta, found in his research that Indian market has always gone down every second year and recovered in the third year. This may not be always true. It is now on record that since 2008 market has not recovered till 2013. But according to expert, despite high inflation and rupee value going down market may turn around by 2016. This is only calculated thinking for nobody can exactly predict the behaviours of stock markt.The market crashed in 2000, 2002, 2004, 2006 & 2008. The market always reached high point before the crash in those years. When market crashed in 2008 again, he predicted that it would surely reach the highest point in 2010. He advised that it would be prudent to wait and stay invested till then. The crash of the equity market is a temporary phenomenon. Hence my advice to my readers is to stay invested and not to panic at all. Rather if you have money, then invest in five—or four-star funds systematically. Go to www. valueresearchonline.com and find best funds.

The country is passing through an economic and political transition. The upward trend of crude price, easy liquidity and non availability of commodities has created an inflationary pressure. At the same time, the political situation of the country is fluid. The Government is also in transition from a principle-driven ally that was blackmailing it to a new unprincipled ally who is perhaps getting ready to extract a pound of flesh. The growth is slowing down. There is a genuine fear in the climate of the country. The only silver lining is timely arrival of the monsoon. A number of investment pundits of Business TV and newspapers have turned fiercely negative. Their consensus view is—"We are doomed!" Under such circumstances, it is natural for the common investing public to enquire: "Should we invest in equity now?" "Should we withdraw our savings from equity?" I am a robust optimist and do not share the negative attitude of business-investment pundits. Rather, I would like to remind you the words of the greatest Investment Guru of the modern world, Warren Buffet: "Common people should feel fearful when others (regular investors) are greedy and they should turn greedy when regular investors are fearful of the equity market." Please keep this in mind—this is the time when the regular investor is feeling fearful. So this is the time, for us common people, to invest systematically and earn a fortune within five years. If anyone would have invested Rs.10, 000 per month under SIP for 120 months, he would have earned more than Rs. 3 crores by now under Reliance Growth (growth option). Do not panic, be patient and stay invested is our advice. You will be the winner!

INVESTMENT IN EQUITY

Investment in equity is the most profitable, next only to investment in art. The return on equity is even higher than the home asset in the long run, which is much higher than the long term return of Gold. But investment in equity is also the most risky. Nobody should invest in equity unless he has the capacity to withstand the shock of volatility. Investment is not child's play, it is a serious business. One of our readers asked me whether he should keep away from the equity market. My reply to him was that if he was not prepared to take short term risk, it would be better to stay away from the share market. The share market is for long term investment only. He asked me: How long is the term?

According to provisions of SEBI, a one year-old investment is considered as a long term investment. But according to me, unless the investor is prepared to wait for at least three to five years, no investment should be done in the equity market. There are people who want to make money overnight. I do not believe that honest money can be made so fast without losing sleep! The equity investment is the most profitable financial avenue. But investment in equity is advisable, provided the investor can handle the risk. Another thing to be kept in mind is that the return from equity investment should be expected at the rate of 20% of the investment only. During the last three years, returns in the Indian stock market were phenomenal. This kind of return is not normal. Before investing, investors must learn that they should expect only 20% return annually, not more. If they earn more it must be their luck and should try to book the profit, unless they have the capacity to withstand risk temporarily. Pertaining to this subject, you can read a book written in Assamese "Honchoi aaru Mitoboyita" (Banolata) for better understanding of the subject.

It is now a well established fact that market moves are determined not only by fundamentals such as profits and sales, but are also significantly influenced by investor behaviour. On many occasions, the market has gone up in investor euphoria. The Indian share market has been going up steadily from end of 2007 till 21st January 2008. The Sensex reached 20,800 points. Then suddenly the market crashed. Those who booked profits were beneficiaries of a high return. Investors who waited for a further rise, lost out as the market fell down by 30%. Now days, the Sense has recovered somehow and is fluctuating between 14,800 and 16,800 points. Most of the pundits feel that the market would remain range-bound for a year and a half. However some of the Investment Gurus felt that Indian equity market would remain dormant for three years and look up only after year 2011. "What should we do now?" asked one of our readers.

My advice is that senior citizens should keep away from the equity market for some time till volatility is over. Once market consolidates, they can enter through mutual fund routes instead of direct participation in the share market. My advice to the younger generation is not to withdraw from equity market if they have an investment. Now, their loss is on the paper only. If they demit now, it would be a real loss. They should hold on to their investment. They have time. If they can remain invested, it would reap benefits for them in the long run. One of my readers asked, "Is this the time to enter the market since market has gone down a lot?" That is a good question. Those who can withstand risk can enter now and remain invested for at least three to five years. There is a possibility to gain higher return. But be cautious. Discuss with your investment consultant and advisor and take an informed decision. Do not go by sentiments. Share market is a hardcore business. No action should be taken on emotional grounds.

What type of shares should be purchased now? If someone wants to buy shares for an investment purpose then it would be prudent to buy those shares whose fundamentals are beyond doubt. Even defensive shares like pharmacy could be thought of. The shares of blue chip companies could be also thought of. My sincere advice is not to trade on shares. People of Assam have just started the investment and savings habits. This is not the time for them to trade on share. Let the investment habit grow over the years. Let investors feel confident and then only enter the field of cash and derivative segments popularly known as futures and options. My sincere advice is to keep away from Share trading now. To make money in share market, people would need patience, boldness and capacity to take temporary risk. Till these attributes are acquired, investors from Assam would do well to keep away from the Share markets.

INVESTORS SHOULD REBALANCE THEIR
PORTFOLIO FROM TIME TO TIME

It is a common complaint that when a mutual fund was purchased two years back it was a five-star fund. It also gets lot of awards from rating agencies. But within one and half years, its performance went down and did not deliver good return. One of our readers purchased SBI Global fund in 2006. For one year it gave excellent return. But from the beginning of 2007 it never looked up. Every day it went down and returns were negligible even during first day of the January 2008 when return of the sensex was at the peak level. What has gone wrong? How to trust a good performing mutual fund? These were the common questions of many investors.

One thing must be kept in mind: Even a good mutual fund may also fall from grace temporarily. It can be for various factors. Some time madcap shares don't perform well. In case the fund has heavy bias on the madcap at that time the funds would not perform well. Sometimes, when the fund manger expecting some kind of movement in the share market changes the pattern of shares but ultimately market did not change then also funds suffer. The successes of the funds depend on the market movements as well as the capabilities of the fund manger. So investors need to observe the movements of the market from time to time.

How often should investors study the movements?

Mutual funds need not be checked on a daily basis. That is the duty of the professional fund manger and not that of an investor. According to me, the movement of the market and the relative performance of the fund to which he subscribe should be checked up once in a year. It is not only necessary, but imperative.

While buying into a mutual fund it should be noted that no new fund needs to be bought just because it is available at Rs. 10 per unit. Mutual funds should be bought on the basis of its past performance. While buying units of a mutual fund, past performance and the consistency of performance should be given the maximum weight. Once upon a time, Franklin's Prima was the star of mutual funds along with its compatriot, Franklin Blue Chips. In 2007, when almost all of their competitors were doing well, both these funds never gave good returns. People felt frustrated. Many investors shifted from the Blue Chip fund to HDFC top 200 or to BN Paribas Select Focus with astounding results. So what should be done?

Our recommendation to investors while buying mutual funds is that they should buy though a good financial advisor who will be ready to help them out and advice them what to do when funds are not doing well. It should be noted that a mutual fund having high NAV may look costly but may give better return. High NAV does not necessarily mean costly units. What investors should look at is the return it has given over the years. While buying mutual funds, investors should diversify the portfolio. Reliance on one particular sector is not desirable. It should include not only equity but also debt instruments. Senior citizens should also buy a balanced fund. The ELSS fund can also be purchased to take dual benefits of return and income-tax benefit. If you can buy a portfolio of Rs. 7500 per month in mutual funds, you would earn 1 crore and 15 lakh within 20 years considering a return of 15%.

Many people have asked us whether ULIP is good. I would like to make it amply clear that ULIP is a product of Insurance and not of investment. ULIP is good for pension benefit or for children's educational purposes backed by safety. One thing must be kept in mind that the portfolio must be rebalanced once a year to get optimum benefit.

How should elders invest?

Senior citizens, looking for safer and better return, may now invest in Medium term gilt fund for a year to earn from 12% to 15%. There would be no income tax but only 10% capital gains tax.

TRACK YOUR INVESTMENTS PERIODICALLY

The investment of money in any asset class is not the end of a story. Your job is half done once you invest in shares and mutual funds. You must track your investments periodically. Why? All the shares and mutual funds do not give you best returns all the time. Sometimes returns are poor and sometime they are very good. You need to check up from time to time as to how your assets are performing. Are your assets giving you good returns? It is not always possible to provide you with great returns. What should investors look for? Should investors look for the best funds only? No, not really. Investors should aim for *consistent* returns. The returns must be risk adjusted. The Blue Chip Fund of Franklin Templeton was one of the best funds once upon a time. It was a five star fund for many years. It remained one of the best funds till 2005. But suddenly it fell from grace and today it is considered as a three star fund. So what should investor do?

Investors should periodically track the performance of their investments. It is not necessary to track investment regularly. Bank Fixed Deposits and small savings funds do not need tracking. Their returns are fixed for all the time. Sometimes, depending on RBI's bank rate and Cash Reserve Ratio, the rate of fixed deposit changes. Till early 2007 most of the Banks used to pay interest of around 10%. Today the interest rate is as low as 8 to 9% for a term deposit of four to five years. But change in rates of interest is rare. Generally term deposits are mostly stable. Once you make an investment in PPF (one of the best investment options in small savings) and MIS of post office you can rest assured. No one needs to track these investments. But you need to keep it in mind that most of the time returns of these instruments cannot beat the rate of inflation. So your investment becomes a losing proposition as your real income goes down. However, due to double benefit of income tax under section 80c and 10 in PPF your investment do provide a decent return without tensions.

Now, some of my readers ask, "In which asset class should they invest regularly and how much?"

The investment is a personal choice. Depending on the (a) availability of funds, (b) on the capacity to take risk and (c) age of the investor, funds should be deployed for investment. In one of our earlier articles I advised that all the eggs should not be kept in one basket. Younger investors (till 40 years) can invest 60% of his investable amount in equity funds and the balance money can be saved in small savings and bank deposit. The investment should be diversified into (1) Bank's term deposits, (2) small savings instruments, (3) mutual funds (equity linked & income fund) and (4) in shares. The greatest investment of course is building a place to live. One of the readers from Duliajan asked, "When should a person start investing in mutual Fund?" Older investors can invest 30% of investable money in equity and the balance in small savings and in bank's FD.

INVESTMENTS MUST BE DIVERSIFIED

It is most essential not to invest money in only one asset class. The investment must be diversified even within one asset class too. It is now an established fact that the best returns on asset is available from equity investment in the long term. But it is too risky to put all the money into equity. The return from equity fluctuates wildly in near term and during the midterm. In 2003, an investor put most of his money (Rs. 1 lakh) and kept the money invested in the same mutual fund till May 2008. He has not lost money—his accounts have a credit balance of Rs. 11 lakh now). If the same person had invested another Rs. 1 lakh in October 2007 in the same fund, his amount would have reduced to Rs. 77,000 as of May 2008. He would have lost almost 30% percent. This example has been given to highlight the volatility of equity investment in short term.

What are the different asset classes, other than equity, where investors need to invest?

The different asset classes where investor can invest money are house property, sculptures & paintings of celebrated artists, Public Provident Fund scheme, small savings schemes, bank fixed deposit, Arbitrage Fund, and Commodity Funds like crude oil, steel, gold and even grains, pulses and cooking oil. Besides equity, Art provides higher rate of returns. It is not house property, as popularly believed!

Where should an investor invest?

Investment is a personal choice. An investor should surely diversify his investment. But the investment portfolio need not be too large. Very often, it becomes too difficult to manage when the portfolio is widely diversified. The best thing to do is to strike a balance depending on your capabilities. The investor should concentrate on at least five large cap shares and two midcap shares of reputed companies. S/he should not invest in more than five mutual funds, out of which three should be diversified (including balanced), one should be ELSS and one could be an income fund. Young investors can indulge in investing 60% of the available funds in an equity-related instrument. But they must invest 40% of their investments in small-savings schemes.

Middle aged investors (person just above 50 years) should bring down his equity investment to 50% and increase the investment in fixed income schemes proportionately. Senior citizen (60 years) should have high fixed income investment (60%) and lower equity-related instruments (40%). As soon as someone reaches 75 years, s/he should avoid investing in equity related instruments (except in Arbitrage Funds) and should concentrate only on fixed deposit of banks and in the long-standing PPF account to avail Income Tax benefit.

Bhupati Hazarika, a well known business executive, opened his account in PPF in 1980. He is still continuing with it. Many people do not know that PPF accounts can be renewed every five years and money can be taken out every year after the seventh year. Bhupati still maintains the PPF account and takes out money from the fund in case of emergency or when he is travelling abroad on holidays. His account gets credited with an almost similar amount the next year when he gets his account updated. During his service life, Bhupati used to deposit Rs. 60,000 annually but now he deposits only Rs. 500 to maintain the continuity of account. (If someone forgets to deposit money in any particular year, he can restart the account by paying a penalty charge of Rs. 100/—only). I strongly recommend that investors who have an old PPF account should continue maintaining the account instead of closing it. It will also diversify their portfolio and help to defend the risk during a volatile time.

While investing, every one must try to study and learn the basics philosophy of investment. This can be done by subscribing to an investment journal and reading books on investment. While some shares respond positively to market triggers, others react negatively. For example, when the price of crude goes up, shares of crude producing companies like ONGC and Reliance also goes up; whereas, shares of automobile manufacturers or ancillaries manufacturers go down. As and when the Indian rupee gains, against the US dollar, the share value of software-exporters generally fall, but the share values of importing companies show a gain. Similarly when interest rates move up, stock of new industries needing finance like motorcycle manufacturers, real-estate builders go down. Yet, companies having surplus funds would gain. So, do we recommend balancing of one stock against another? I do not. It is more of a theory. To me, investment is mostly a gut feeling. To make money you need to take a calculated risk. So, diversify your portfolio, stay invested for long term and get a decent return.

FIXED MATURITY PLANS ARE AGAIN FLAVOUR OF THE MARKET

In the investment horizon there are many plans to invest your money in the market. There are equity funds, index funds, debt funds, ELSS and fixed-maturity funds. Among all the funds, fixed-maturity funds are less risky. One thing to be kept in mind is that fixed-maturity funds are not risk proof as generally made out to be. They, however, are next best to fixed deposit in a bank, PPF, and SCSS, as far as security of money is concerned. A Fixed-Maturity Plan protects capital but is open to interest rate risk. It provides better return most of the time than a fixed deposit. This fund is popularly known as FMP.

The reason investors choose FMPs is for their high returns which are also indicated but not guaranteed. In order to give assured returns, FMPs opt for very secure investment options like AAA rated corporate bonds whose maturity tenure matches the maturity tenure of the FMP. However in the recent times, some of these FMPs started investing in commercial paper from real estate and finance companies, in order to give higher returns to their investors.

The investing in FMPs allows an investor to earn higher returns while minimizing their exposure to the risk. As a result, many fund houses have introduced their FMPs to entice investors to invest with them. But what are FMPs? Are they safe as they seem to be? If not, what are their pitfalls? We explained in the beginning of the article about the myth surrounding the FMPs. It is not always safe like Bank FDAs as the name implies; these plans have a certain maturity period. They are close-ended funds; meaning, you can invest in them only when they are open for purchase. This is only during the NFO period. To redeem your investment, you need to wait for the pan to mature or pay a stiff 2% exit load. Generally FMPs are for a period of around 13-18 months. In case you can survive the period, a handsome gain can be expected. If you take your money out during midstream you lose money as there is high exit load.

How can FMPs provide a better return than a bank FD?

In order to give assured returns, FMPs opt for very secure investment options like AAA rated corporate bonds whose maturity tenure matches the maturity tenure of FMP. It is however a myth that there is no risk in FMP. Despite their claims of being one of the safest investment options around, FMPs do have their own share of risks. A few of them are as under:

Those FMPs offering a higher yield can afford to do so by investing in comparatively risky investment options. This has been evident in 2008, when these funds faced a liquidity crisis due to their exposure to real estate and finance companies. In recent times, some of the FMPs started investing in commercial paper from real estate and finance companies, in order to give higher returns to their investors. When the finance and realty companies landed in trouble during the recent economic downturn, their offerings also lost value. Investors pulled out in panic. With the investors pulling out their investments from these FMPS, the funds were forced to offload their investments in the illiquid markets, thereby causing a liquidity crisis. But ultimately investors who stayed invested did not loose at the end of the period and got almost assured returns. The actual yield will depend on the yield of the debt instruments at the time of actually investing your money. In reality, FMPs offer safety of their capital, but they do not offer protection against interest rate risk. As the interest rate rises, the value of the bonds goes down. This sometime can affect the returns of the fund.

What precautions should investors take while opting for FMPs?

To get the best out of an FMP certain precautionary measures should be taken. Always check the indicative portfolio of the funds. In case you find any non-AAA security avoid that particular FMP. The assured yields are based on the indicative yield. Do not confuse this with a guarantee. Sometime there are wide gaps between the yield shown while launching and the actual yield at the time maturity. Sometime it is more but sometimes it can go lower. The golden rule is to stick to the maturity period of the plan. Don't withdraw halfway through as it will force the fund manager to redeem investments at any available price, thereby causing losses to you as well as other investors. The FMPs are good investments for risk-averse people of the middle-age group. But do not put all the eggs in one basket. You can put 10% of the total investment in a fixed maturity plan and earn better return compared to the Fixed Deposit of a bank.

CHAPTER SEVEN

Pension, Credit Cards, Pan Card and Unemployment

PRIVATE SECTOR EMPLOYEES AND
THE SELF-EMPLOYED NEED A PENSION PLAN

There was a time when no one in Northeast thought of contributing to a pension fund during their career. They were almost unconcerned of their retirement needs. Only the government employees used to get pension that made their life easier compared to other professionals. Even the teachers of schools and colleges never got pension. Large companies would have a Contributory Provident Fund and Gratuity and most of them were never paid pension. Only a handful of multi-national companies contributed to a pension fund managed by independent trust and LIC. Many of our readers have asked as to how important pension funds are and whether all the wage earners should try to subscribe to a New Pension Scheme launched by the Government of India during May Day a few years back. They want to know whether government pension is better or the schemes launched by private and public sector insurers and mutual funds are better.

I would like to advise that all wage earners should be members of a pension scheme of their choice for it helps in making their life easier and secure. Most people fail to think of pension plans during their youth. But as time progresses, they realize the importance of pension. To be frank, pension by the government to its employees is a boon. Nowadays, besides officials and clerical staff, teachers of aided colleges and provincial's schools get pension and they are a much happier lot. The government's pension plan was an inflation-neutral product and was a great scheme. However, the old system has been replaced by the new scheme that is only a contribution oriented pension scheme.

Besides the Government, LIC has a few individual-oriented pension schemes like Jeevan Dhaara. SBI Life, ICICI and HDFC also have their own pension schemes based on annuity payment. But by far the best pension scheme for the "Aam Janata" or individual wage-earners is the New Pension Scheme launched last year. Surprisingly, there are not many takers of this great scheme. I am sure in the long run people will realize its necessity and will surely subscribe. This new plan is great for the middle class and could make life a lot easier after retirement. Franklin Templeton is the only mutual fund which has a debt oriented pension scheme.

The new voluntary pension scheme came into force in India with young people as its main target. It hoped to reach out to 87 percent of the nation's workforce that remained uncovered by any retirement benefit. The Pension Fund Regulatory and Development Authority extended the scheme on May Day a few years back to all citizens, after introducing it to fresh recruits of the central government since Jan 1, 2004. It took 10 years of conceptualisation.

Under the new scheme, beneficiaries can divide their investments in three categories. These can be in equity, government securities and corporate bonds and mutual funds.

According to the PRD Authority, one can opt to invest only 50 percent of the funds in equity, which will be in index funds of the Bombay Stock Exchange and the National Stock Exchange. It can be 100 percent for the other two categories. Contributions will be made towards two accounts, one of which will be entirely for savings towards retirement, which cannot be withdrawn. The other portion will be voluntary and can be encashed whenever the beneficiary pleases.

The second portion, however, takes effect only six months after joining the scheme, for which the eligibility is 18-55 years. Those who join will be allotted a permanent retirement account number so that the account can be operated from anywhere. Beneficiaries can exit the scheme after reaching 60 years of age. They can continue only up to the time they are 70.

According to the regulatory authority, out of the estimated 425 million-strong workforce in the country, as many as 370 million were still not covered under any pension scheme. Twenty years down the line, it is expected that the majority of them will be covered, but the current position is very low.

Officials at the regulatory authority said that Rs. 2,100 crore (Rs. 21 billion or $420 million) stood invested in the new pension scheme for central-government employees, giving an annual rate of return of an impressive 12-16%. This return is very decent when compared to debt fund-based pension scheme. There is also a good pension scheme in the mutual fund domain but the New Pension Fund initiated by the government seems better, even though there are not enough takers for unknown reasons. Perhaps this scheme needs to be marketed much more aggressively.

Six pension-fund managers have been appointed by the regulators for the new scheme, with 22 points of reference—the institutions that beneficiaries can approach to join. The persons willing to join the scheme can approach nationalized banks and large private banks for applications forms. Upon registration, between the ages of 18-55 years, a person will receive a Permanent Retirement Account Number. The minimum contribution is Rs. 6,000 per annum. The money has to be paid in at least four instalments a year. No instalment can be of less than Rs. 500. There is no upper limit on the number of instalments or the money one can put in per instalment.

The account will be closed in the event of the death of the account holder, when the account value reduces to zero, or with changes in citizenship status. The subscribers can also exit the policy before 60 years provided he or she annuitizes at least 80 percent of the corpus. The self initiated pension is a new concept and could be greatly beneficial to subscribers. If a person fails to contribute the minimum instalment in a year then s/he would have to bear a default penalty of Rs. 100 per year of default and the account will become dormant. In order to reactivate the account, pay the minimum contributions, along with penalty due. A dormant account will be closed when the account value falls to zero. NPS is a defined contribution scheme and the benefits will depend upon the amounts contributed and the investment growth up to the point of exit from NPS. It should be clearly understood that as with every investment, there is a degree of risk under NPS also. The value of investment in NPS may rise or fall, but investment in equity will be a maximum of 50% or lower. It would be like a balanced fund. You should be able to advise a minimum exposure to equity.

In case someone starts their contribution to NPS at 30 years of age they would need a pension purse of Rs. 319,000 (at today's prices) at the age of 60 to get a pension of Rs. 2,000 per month. To realise this, they would need to contribute approximately Rs. 16,600 every year or Rs. 1350/—per month. If, a person contributes Rs. 6000/—per month, he is expected to get a return of Rs. 10,000/—every month, after he reaches sixty years. So carry with the NPS till 70 and get around Rs. 20,000/—or more per month. This is a conservative calculation. You may get more depending on the market conditions at the time of retirement. Pensioners also have an option of selecting an annuity which will pay the survivor the pension of their spouse.

THE NEW PENSION SCHEME HAS BROUGHT CHEERS FROM THE PUBLIC

The New Pension Scheme announced by the government a couple of years back was first announced for the employees of Government of India only. Now any citizen of India is able to join the scheme and plan their livelihood after retirement. This, however, is not the only pension scheme in the country. In fact, before this scheme was introduced, there were two distinct pension schemes in existence. The first one was from insurance companies and the second one was from mutual-fund houses. Then why was everyone waiting eagerly for this plan to be introduced?

There are a few reasons. In India, people generally tend to believe the Government more than the private sector. Secondly, the new pension scheme is simple. Thirdly, it is cost effective. Fourthly, it is managed by experts and has incorporated checks and balances so that citizens do not lose heavily when money is required most.

The scheme envisages that at a younger age, more investment should be made in equity. Slowly as the citizens grow older, more investment would be diverted to government bonds and fixed deposit of banks, etc. This would ensure low volatility. Even with such checks and balances it is not possible to predict the exact return, as the investments would be market—linked. In this connection it would be worth mentioning that employees in the organized sector already have 'employee's pension scheme' where employers and employees contribute 8.33% and 3.67% respectively of the salary. The return from the scheme is pretty low. The new scheme provides for a better return as part of the money is invested in the equity market. However, it will be possible to take out the invested money only when the citizen reaches the retirement age of sixty years. Upon retirement, the entire contribution of subscribers will be put under an annuity scheme to enable them to get a monthly pension. In exceptional circumstances, contributions can be taken out before retirement but 80% of the money shall have to be put in an annuity scheme.

The regulators have classified investments under three categories—E, G, and C, from which citizens are able to choose their portfolio. E-class asset means high return and high risk indicating equity participation through index funds. Under the G asset class, the investment is restricted to government bonds. Under the C-asset class, investments will be made into a liquid fund of MF, fixed deposits of banks, etc. In case of government employees, a mere 5% of their funds can be invested in equity, whereas for general citizens up to 50% investment can be made in the stock market. If citizens want, they can leave the investment choice to fund managers. This system is known as *auto-choice*.

Who can join the scheme? Any Indian citizen between 18 and 55 years would be able to subscribe to the scheme. At present, only tier-I of the scheme, involving a contribution to a non-withdraw able account is open. Subsequently, tier-II accounts, which permit voluntary savings that can be withdrawn at any point of time, can be opened. But to be eligible to open a tier-II account, you need a tier-I account. To enrol, subscribers will need to visit a point of presence (PoP) and fill up the prescribed form with the required documents. Once you are registered, the Central Recordkeeping Agency (CRA) will send you a Permanent Retirement Account Number (PRAN), along with telephone and internet passwords. There is no investment ceiling. But the minimum investment limit has been fixed at Rs. 500 a month or Rs. 6,000 annually. Subscribers are required to contribute at least once a quarter but there is no ceiling on how many times you invest during the year. Subscribers will have to bear a penalty of Rs. 100 per year of default and will need to pay it with the minimum amount to reactivate the account. Also, dormant accounts will be closed when the account value falls to zero. A friend asked me is there any guarantee? My reply was: No. There is no guarantee since NPS is a defined contribution scheme and the benefits depend on the amount contributed and the investment growth up to the time of exit.

At the moment, the Pension Fund Regulatory and Development Authority (PFRDA) has selected six fund managers—State Bank of India, UTI, ICICI Prudential, Kotak Mahindra, IDFC and Reliance— on the basis of a bidding and technical evaluation process. What happens if someone shifts out of the city where s/he has started the NPS? The PRAN remains the same and you can access a toll-free number (1-800-222080). The details of your PRAN and details of transactions will be available on the CRA website: (www.npscra.nsdl. co.in).

I believe that the new pension scheme is a good instrument and people who are professionals and working independently like journalists, advocates, doctors, consultants, singers, artists, and small-business owners may find it useful. It is up to individual persons and their appetite for risk which will determine whether to buy shares or to subscribe to NPS. We welcome the new scheme, for its risk-adjusted profile.

CREDIT CARD DEFAULT CAN BE
REALISED FROM SALARY NOW

Credit-card defaults have now reached such a limit that a new legal provision has been put in effect to realise the dues from the salary of cardholders. With the new provision, defaulting card holders have to be very cautious to protect their money and reputation. Defaulting credit card holders may risk their credit worthiness too. Of course, it is also true that most credit card companies used to collect, at the slightest pretext, their outstanding dues by applying strong-arm tactics. There were volleys of protests against such uncivilised behaviour of the credit card companies. Fortunately, the courts barred these companies from using force and extra-legal provisions but it also equipped the banks with a legal provision to realise their legal dues from card holders.

What really is a credit card? What is its function? A credit card is a small plastic card that is part of a system of payments issued to users by the banking system. It is a card entitling its holder to buy goods and services based on the holders promise to pay for these goods and services. The issuer of the card grants a line of credit to the consumer (or the user) from which the user can borrow money for payment to a merchant or as a cash advance to the user, to be paid within a specific period of time as agreed. The working class should be aware that from now onwards, credit-card defaults can be realised directly from your salary payment.

The use of credit cards is like a double-edged sword. When used judiciously and with good intention, it is helpful to users. When used recklessly, it creates problems for the users. The payment of credit cards must be made in time. Though a credit card allows payment to be made slowly or partially, this facility should not be availed by salaried persons as it is a very costly option. The interest charged for the outstanding dues is generally more than 40%! The money kept in fixed deposits of banks nowadays earns a maximum interest rate of 9%. It is obvious that even if a credit card is used, the money should be paid immediately on receipt of the bill to be cost effective.

Recently, two very important steps were taken with respect to credit cards that all card users need to know. Firstly, as I already mentioned, in case of credit card default, the money can be deducted from the salary of the card holder. Secondly, a PIN number has been introduced to protect card holders from fraud.

Perhaps, by now most credit card holders know that a separate PIN number is required to use the credit card online. This provision came in force as per the directive of RBI. Now it is the responsibility of the credit card holders to apply for this PIN number from their respective banks. This method has been adopted so that any form of fraud can be avoided. The credit card number could be stolen, copied and can remembered, but the PIN number will only be known to the individual concerned. This concept has been introduced to ensure another layer of security. It is no longer possible to complete a credit card transaction online without this individual PIN number or password.

Some credit-card users forget to pay their bills on time and their outstanding amount multiplies fast. Upon default of the original and subsequent dues, credit card issuers keep on sending reminders and if no response is received the holders then deploy recovery agents, who are actually a gang of hoodlums, to realise the due payments. In such a situation, credit card users face harassment and sometimes may suffer physical assault besides experiencing a traumatic situation.

It is often seen that the younger generation, in their zeal to show off their purchasing power, flash out their credit cards to buy goods and commodities but later fail to pay, thereby inviting unnecessary trouble for themselves. A few years back, an incident took place in Guwahati that highlights the misuse of a credit card. There were a group of friends who, after graduating, found jobs in a few multinational companies selling different products. After their office hours, these friends would meet almost every evening in a fast-food joint near Christian Basti in G.S. Road to have some innocent fun. Rajib Bharadwaz and Dhiraj Borah, in the group, were two friends working in the same company. One evening when all the friends assembled, Rajib's business acumen was discussed and everyone congratulated him for fulfilling his annual sales target within six months. Rajib told his friends that by the year's end he would get a special bonus for his achievement. The initial congratulations slowly changed into pressure to throw a dinner party that night itself. Rajib agreed to a party the next week since he had no cash in his pocket that night. But his friends were unrelenting and kept on demanding the party that night itself. Ultimately, Dhiraj, his colleague, agreed to use his credit card with an assurance that Rajib would pay him the money next week. Everyone enjoyed the party and all the friends thanked Rajib.

In due course, when the bill came Rajib was away on tour. Upon his return Dhiraj gave him the bill and asked him to deposit the money next day as he was going out on tour. Rajib kept the bill with him and forgot to send the payment to the credit card company. The due date of payment expired and the credit card issuer kept on sending reminders. When the company did not receive payment for three months, recovery agents arrived at Dhiraj's home. They insulted his parents and forced them not only to pay the amount but to hand over their fees as penalty. The parents were shaken. Dhiraj was a regular bill-payer. He took up the matter with the bank but not much could be achieved. Dhiraj only then realised the danger of using a credit card on emotional grounds. He realised it was not correct to flash out the credit card to pay someone else's dues. It was also not correct for him to hand over the bill for payment to someone else. He should have asked for the money as decided and paid the bill himself. For his own fault, he lost his money and a friend. When the realisation came to him, it was already too late.

The above incident is a true story. All young people should realise that credit and debit cards are sacred instruments to be used with utmost care. It is not meant for making any style or fashion statement. Please don't let your credit and debit card numbers be known to anyone. In another incident, Jyoti Basu, the erstwhile CM of West Bengal, was shaken when his debit card was stolen by his security man and used. The person concerned was later nabbed. So use your credit card, ATM card and debit card with utmost caution.

Over the years, the news of banks using muscle men in the garb of recovery agents reached the Reserve Bank of India but no substantial steps were taken. The court delivered a judgment that banks would be in their right to recover their outstanding credit card bills if payments remain due for long. They can take legal means to recover their dues but will not be able to use brutal force. The recovery agents will have no right to talk to anyone other than the holder of the card. Despite these legal sanctions, many people failed to make timely payment of their credit card bills and the banks felt frustrated as it led to large losses. Recently, a provision was made by the bank whereby if any employed person does not pay the credit card dues on time, it would be possible for the banks to realise the amount from the salary of the person concerned. Now employed person should be aware of this provision. This not only would lead to the realisation of money from their salary, but they may have to suffer defamation. Their credit rating may go down and ultimately it might create a black spot in their career. This fact was kept secret till now. The matter came to light when a bank started using the provision legally.

ICICI bank is the first bank to utilise this concept. While issuing credit cards, they bind the holders in such a way that in case payments are not received during the due dates, the bank is in a position to approach their employers and legally deduct the dues from their salary. This provision would be made legally foolproof and others banks are also expected to follow the rule when issuing credit card to the holders.

Many educated people were also under the impression that dues of credit cards can be avoided. But as the days passed by, the non payment of credit card dues have been taken as a legal offense. Nowadays, the provision of taking debt has become easier but for that the credit rating of individuals has become very important. From now on, before sanctioning housing credit and car loans, the banks would check the credit rating of an individual. In most of the developed countries such provisions are most essential. In India, up till now, loans were easily available for the working group. But now onwards, credit rating will become necessary. So every young person must zealously protect their credit status from now onward by preventing misuse of their credit cards. It must be kept in mind that a default in credit card payment not only brings you a bad name but may also destroy your credit worthiness. So, beware of credit card default. Regular payers of credit card would have great advantage in building their credit worthiness.

HOW TO GENERATE EMPLOYMENT AND INCOME

Sad news is hitting Indian society all the time since January 2008. In a period of recession the worst affected area is always the industrial sector. This sector always becomes the first to receive social bullets during a downturn. Since industrial enterprises, in the period of a boom, create employment liberally, it gets affected badly during the time of economic recession. In India, agriculture is the biggest employer. It is followed by the textile industry. Due to falling exports more than four lakh employees lost jobs during the recession. This has a cascading effect. Most employees were blue-collar workers. Up until then sophisticated urban boys were losing jobs. Then skilled workers started losing jobs. These forces inevitably create turmoil in society. Should this trend continue chaos may erupt resulting in arson and looting which has never been seen in our society as a result of economic depression. Even during the Bengal famine no such upheaval occurred amongst the various socioeconomic segments.

President Barrack Obama recently forewarned the youth of America that unless they were prepared to compete with Chinese and Indian youth, they might be annihilated. Mediocrity would be neither be tolerated nor survived. The American youth needs to pull up their socks in case they want to survive. These words of President Obama were meant for the young men and women of his country. But they are true for our own country also. Our youth must develop skills, new skills for new jobs. Development of skills alone would not resolve our problems. Indian workers will have to understand the dignity of labour.

In a time of recession, the service sector might be the only answer for most new workers. The service sector needs honest and dedicated employees. Over the years we have seen how the transport sector has developed with private drivers providing excellent service. Ten years back, 12 continuous hours of dedicated service from employees was unthinkable. Now it has become the order of the day. Courier services are another example of dedicated service.

During a recession, it is health—and food-related industries which can provide some stability. In this respect, the government can help by providing training facilities for health-related machines and instruments. The medical facilities of private sector enterprises can be utilized for training purposes. These boys could be deployed after proper training to the villages to take care of the health of the population.

Perhaps, development of the agriculture sector could also be a saviour. In Assam, fertility of the land is high but credit availability is low. Except in a few places, supply of fertilizers and irrigational canals are not sufficient. The government can focus these areas for development. This is also the time to build up roads in villages linking them to the district headquarters. Fisheries are another area where development would be welcome. These are the areas where our youth also have to show interest. Otherwise, money spent by our government will go to the new generation of workers across the border.

The Government must also start quasi-medical facilities at the earliest. A host of engineering colleges have been opened. There will be a requirement for laboratory technicians, teachers, demonstrators, etc. Our students must also be prepared to accept training and get retrained in media-related avenues. Usually, during these times there is no chance of losing jobs in media, educational institutes, nursing, and NGOs. More and more services are coming into the fore in NGOs. The social welfare segments are also coming up pretty well. Instead of waiting endlessly for the job postings, which they were promised during campus interviews, young engineers should prepare for All India Civil Service jobs. A lot of engineers are required in the defence forces. Young graduates can keep their eyes and ears open and apply for these job. In Assam, most of our graduates did not like to compete for Government of India jobs. Slowly this trend seems to be changing. The most important thing during these periods is the support of family. Family members must try to provide a great deal of support to the youth who have not been able to get jobs or have been laid off. The unions of the state also have a role to play. Instead of always confronting the management it is time to cooperate with the management. Productivity must not be ignored. Lay-offs can be avoided at the cost of accepting a lower salary if need be. One thing must be kept in mind that bad times will not continue for ever. It is bound to change. These bad days will change for good. Workers must wait with positive outlook.

RECEIPIENT OF GIFTS SHALL HAVE TO PAY TAX

"Can I gift my house to my daughter?" asked one worried father. He learnt that the Gift Tax rules had changed and now the government intends to charge a high tax on the recipients of gifts. "My daughter is not earning much. How will she pay tax on an immovable property?" The latest gift tax amendment has created tension in the minds of lots of senior citizens. I would like to assure you that gifts from blood relations are exempt from the tax even now.

The Government of India amended the Gift Tax only because the provision was misused by unscrupulous people. High Value Gifts were a safe haven to show one's love to others, financially. Now the tax man has tightened (putting it mildly) the strings attached to gifts. In fact, the rule has become so tight that it may be the end for all high value gifts in India.

Since 1998, there is no Gift Tax per se in India. The gift is now added to the income of the receiver and is taxed accordingly. Earlier (prior to October 1, 2009), gifts in kind (a car or a house) were not considered at their cash value. Many rich and powerful people would request some of their friends and associates to give expensive gifts during their daughter's marriage in lieu of big favours. At that time, all gifts received during marriage were exempt from tax. The gifts could have been from anyone and of any type. This made very high value gifts the norm in marriages of very powerful and rich people. The taxman was hoodwinked by making these marriages an occasion for large-scale conversion of illegal money (black money) into legal gifts. This system was rampant. The government knew but had no courage to stop it. Ultimately, Mr. Man Mohan Singh's government mustered enough courage and made a provision to stop it with a new rule.

What is the new rule? The change in the rule related to gifts now says that the receiver has to pay tax for receiving any gift valued at Rs. 50,000 or more. The "any gift" clause includes not only cash but all gifts of any value. So, if someone receives the gift of a house worth Rs. 30 lakhs, then s/he is automatically in the highest income bracket and has to pay 30% + surcharge on the value of the house as tax (close to Rs. 10 lakhs in this case). It is obviously very difficult for a young girl with limited means to pay such a high rate of income tax if she is not officially very rich. The rule, thus, effectively prevents money laundering in the guise of high value gifts.

The question now is whether gifts given by relatives in weddings would also attract so much tax? Genuine people do not have to worry at all. There is an exemption for gifts received from certain people. The gifts that one receives from relatives on the occasion of marriage, gifts received from parents and grandparents, gifts received by a daughter-in-law from her parents-in-law, and gifts received by way of a will and inheritance are exempted. But here is a catch. To stop the evil practice of dowry, gifts received by a son-in-law from his parents-in-law will be taxed. Will it bring down demands of dowry? "Very unlikely," said a social scientist. According to him, the demand would stay not in white but in another colour. The father-in-laws will remain as vulnerable as they were before. But a good provision has been made for children living abroad. They can freely send money to their old parents without attracting any gift tax for their parents. Due to existence of this provision, NRIs can gift their parents in India from their NRE account without their parents having to suffer any tax.

An excellent provision has been made so that no one can circumvent the rules. The gifts received in the names of one's minor children will be clubbed with the parents' income for taxation purposes. Also, the taxman is very alert in saying that, in case of both parents having income, clubbing will be done with that parent who is earning more. So one cannot hide under the cover of their minor child(ren) receiving the gifts. For a long time, non-relatives were sending gifts in the name of the minor children and most of the time it was clubbed with the income of the mother so that minimal tax is paid. With the incorporation of the new provision, the loopholes have been plugged.

Not only gifts, but any real estate deal done for values lower than the state government's fixed rates will also be taxed. Here the tax will be charged on the difference between the state government's rate and purchase price. The tax needs to be paid by the buyer of the property. According to a taxation expert, the tightening of the rules related to gift tax will curb money laundering to a great extent. However, it does protect genuine gifts from relatives and loved ones. Several guises used earlier to cover up transactions as gifts are now taxable.

CHAPTER EIGHT

Economic Growth, Miscellaneous Advisory and Intelligent Investing

THE INDIAN ECONOMY IS TURNING AROUND FOR GROWTH

Despite political uncertainty, the Indian economy has been on the path of recovery from the recession. The engine for this growth is not the IT sector but the traditional basic sectors of steel and cement. In the months following the recession, a sudden robust performance of consumer and capital goods, a key barometer of activity, showed that there is generation of demand in the country. In view of the above activities, the Government of India is insisting on a greater say in conducting the affairs of the IMF and the World Bank. If India's political climate turns stable there is a strong possibility for her to don an aggressive new role in these world bodies soon. The short-term outlook for the economy has improved significantly. But there is a glaring lack of faith in the longer term. The lack of consistent growth in industrial production is a pointer in this regard.

The recent data made available to us revealed that demand in India's hinterland is firm and is supporting a vast expanse of the economy. Cement sales have grown at near double-digit rates. The consumer goods sales have seen strong support from rural markets. Auto demand has firmed up and grown, and many auto companies are introducing new models of cars including European manufactures like Fiat,

Volkswagen, and Mercedes or Chevrolet and Ford from the U.S. In the recovery period following the recession, many analysts opined that the robust growth in steel and cement sales as well as in manufacturing in showed that the worst might be over for the economy. However, more than four years later, it is still a matter of debate.

Wholesale price inflation indicated that demand had not fallen as anticipated and prices were holding firm. Despite such firm signals for growth, unemployment may not go down as the younger population is growing every year. The traditional industries have not been great employers. The generation of employment was faster in the IT, garment, gems and jewellery, and service sectors, which are yet to grow at a desired level. Industrial output, which accounts for nearly a quarter of India's gross domestic product, has shown signs of recovery.

Of late, a few economists, felt that stimulus packages brought in by the government since the downturn, along with aggressive policy easing by the central bank, appears to be making an impact, coupled with improved car sales and uptrend in cement and steel demand. It is worth noting that savings and investment rates have reached close to 40 percent due to the structural changes in the economy. This would be able to sustain an investment rate of 35 percent. The last few years have made it quite clear that NRIs are sending more money than before and the foreign exchange reserves may slowly improve.

Here is what we reported and predicted in the months following the recession of 2008:

The main stock index has gone up by more than 40% from its low of early March. FII bought $1.5 billion worth of shares in April and another $296 million recently, after heavy outflows in January and February. However my views are that the sensitive index is still not stable and share market may go further down. My gut feeling is that the index may go further down to around 10,000 levels or below should political stability keep faltering in the coming weeks and months. Investors should be ready to accept the opportunity for long term investment.

According to the well-known rating agency ICRA, the economy is likely to grow 6.5 to 7.5 percent in 2009/10 if the global economy comes out of the slump later this year. But according to us, the growth rate may not come up soon. We had forecasted earlier that Indian's growth would remain below 6.5% during the year. We stand by our forecast as the government stimulus would take time to affect the broader economy of the country. However, there is a strong possibility that by 2010 the Indian economy will recover at a faster speed. We strongly feel that the high fiscal deficit of central and state governments, which according to some observers has reached nearly 10 percent of the gross domestic product, could prove to be an obstacle to growth and undermine the Reserve Bank's aggressive rate cuts. Yet there is a silver lining in the sky. Monsoon is expected to be normal which might trigger better growth and possibilities of lower unemployment.

I will leave the interpretation of the last few years to you and simply state two points: 1. The Indian economy can grow and manifest its potential only if there is political stability, growth oriented fiscal policy, and infrastructure development. All are challenges we had then and all are challenges we still have now. 2. No talk of the Indian economy will ever be complete without a behavioural prediction of our fickle-minded monsoon.

INVESTMENTS TO MATCH FINANCIAL GOALS

"How much should I invest now?" a relative asked me once.

"Why do you want to invest?" I asked him in return.

"There is no reason in particular. Everyone is investing. Market is going up and up. I need to make some money too," he replied.

I advised him not to invest then. I told him to hold on for a while. The market was near an all time high. It would not make good sense to invest at that point. People should not have a "herd mentality" while investing. Investment is a serious business and people should deploy their hard-earned money when the market is down and is ready for a turnaround. It is not a good enough reason that he should invest because everyone was investing. In fact investing should be commensurate with individual financial goals.

How should financial goals be determined?

Financial goals differ from person to person. Depending on age and responsibility financial goals would differ. A young man of a rich father may not have much domestic responsibility. Another son having a widowed mother and younger sister would have responsibility of the family. The financial goals for both these young men would be different. The financial goals of people are always dictated by the circumstances of the family and their relation with the family. Their willingness to share responsibilities would play the most important role. Sometimes people get sandwiched between their responsibilities toward old parents and their children while balancing their financial goals. "Depending on financial goals, when should a person plan for investment?" My reply is: As soon as you start earning.

Saving is not for the faint of heart. It is not child's play. It is easier to earn but difficult to save. It is much more difficult to invest. Of course, in the beginning you cannot save for all you have dreamt in life. If there is a family to look after, it is best to buy a Term Insurance on joining the job. It is cheap and will provide security to your family. Surely, you have a bank account. Your first investment should be in PPF. Alternatively, you can try to maximize your contribution in your PF account. Slowly, after a year, you can try to draw up a plan for financial goals. (At this point of time, you should invest in an ELSS mutual fund that would give you a higher return and also a tax rebate and no capital-gains tax). Perhaps, your sister's marriage, brother's education, and mother's health will get precedence over your own marriage. You can then think of your marriage, a home loan and the plan for a pension fund, if you are not a government servant. After marriage, you need to plan for your children's education and for holidays. You can increase your insurance at that time. With the basic financial plan in place, you need to consult a certified financial advisor and keep investing slowly as per plan. This way you will be the winner.

Please do not be in a hurry to invest. Investment should be done after lots of thinking. Invest only in a good fund that provides risk-adjusted return. State Bank, Reliance Mutual Fund, HDFC fund, HSBC fund, DSPML fund, Kotak and ICICI mutual funds are a few good funds you can rely on. If you need help, go to a good place like Standard Chartered Bank near Rabindra Bhaban, Eastern Financiers Ltd., HDFC Mutual Fund at G. S. Road, or to SBI, in Panbazar. They have excellent investment officers. They can help you know about the best funds. Don't try to buy NFO thinking it is cheap. Buy only four star or five star funds as recommended by Value Research. You can buy funds with a growth option or with a dividend option. Invest an amount which you would not need for at least three years. Recently, one of my readers called up and expressed his willingness to invest Rs. 5 lakh. I asked him for how long he can spare the money. He replied for six months, since the money is required in February 2008. I advised him not to invest. Had he invested in October he would have lost almost 30%. No money should be invested for the short term. Invest only to match financial goals. It is imperative for investors to study books on investment. We would refer to a few books in our next article.

REVERSE MORTGAGE A BOON TO ELDERS

Radhika Baruva, a senior citizen, was really worried about inflation! He had a decent job during his service career. He retired at the age 58 and is around 70 years old now. He planned well. There were no mutual funds during his service career. What he could save was invested in the post office MIS and bank fixed deposits. Due to continuing inflation, his hard-earned money was devalued. Income tax took a further 10% of his earned income. He was really at his wits end balancing his expenditure with his income. He lost his son long back during the war with Pakistan. He does not have to support anyone except his wife. His daughter, happily married, helps him in organizing his life. Yet he remains, of late, under tension all the time.

"Why are you so worried most of the time?" His neighbour Dr. Gogoi asked him once.

"Not really," Baruva replied.

"Are you sure? I am not only your neighbour but also a doctor. If you are not feeling well, I can examine you without obligation!"

"Thank you, Doctor. I am perfectly fine. I had an executive medical check-up the other day and found my pressure is under control and my blood sugar is within the limit."

"Then tell me frankly, what is eating you up?"

Baruva told him that it was not his health but his wealth which is causing him sleepless nights. The doctor replied jokingly "If you have a problem with spending money, I can spend it for you. If you have a problem of keeping it, you can throw it to my compound and I will make good use of it." It was the honest humour of a friendly neighbour. But suddenly Dr. Gogoi noticed a trickle of tears in the eyes of Baruva. The doctor felt embarrassed.

"I am sorry if I have hurt you," said the doctor. The old gentleman explained it was not the problem of excess but of having too little. He was unable to cope up with inflation. Everything is getting so much costlier. He had been unable to paint his house for the last six years. He has not taken a break for the last seven years. Electricity has become so costly that air conditioners remain shut. He cannot afford gasoline, so his old car remains mostly in the garage. It doesn't see daylight unless his daughter visits him. He didn't have a mobile and he had disconnected the STD facility of his landline. Now, he is not sure whether his money in the bank will keep their body and soul together. Sometimes he felt that perhaps it would be impossible to lead an honourable life. Last year, the boys of his neighbourhood came asking for a Bihu donation. He paid them Rs. 50 only against their demand of Rs. 200. "I was unable to pay more. They did not accept the money and threw it back at me and left." He felt insulted but helpless. During Bihu celebrations he remained at home. He was not in a position to visit the *pandal*. His self-respect prevented him.

The doctor realized his plight and took him to an investment advisor. The young investment advisor asked him not to worry. He visited his house and inspected the property. It was a large well-built Assam-type house with a sprawling lawn, kitchen garden and an outhouse. He told him that the government of India has started a Reverse Mortgage scheme under which he can earn a good amount of money monthly to meet his expenses. "How can I repay a mortgage at this age?" asked Baruva. The investment advisor told him that he did not need to pay back. Initially, only the National Housing Board used to give the amount as a loan. But nowadays many banks including State Bank and Punjab National Bank are happy to provide monthly payments against the mortgage of the house. The owner can continue to live in the house till his death. "What about my wife? She is much younger to me," Baruva enquired. She can also continue to live IN THE HOUSE TILL HER DEATH, replied the Advisor. Only after the death of both husband and wife will the property go to the bank. The first offer to buy the property would be given to his daughter. If she refuses, then it will be sold at the market price. After realizing the principal and interest amount, the balance money would be paid to his daughter.

"How much shall we get monthly?" Baruva asked the advisor. "Your house will be valued at Rs. 60 lakhs. You will get 80% of that amount, i.e. Rs. 48 lakhs for a span of 15 years. You will get Rs. 25,000 every month. Will that be sufficient for both of you?" Baruva smiled and said that the amount would be more than sufficient. They would be comfortable and even make a trip to Tirupati temple. Baruva thanked the doctor and the investment advisor for their help. The scheme not only brought him peace of mind but helped them to live with dignity. He visited SBI next day to finalise the deal.

INVESTMENTS DURING HIGH INFLATION

Everyone is talking about inflation now. Inflation has become a part of our life. A few years ago I visited Austria. While walking on a road in Vienna I asked a shopkeeper the price of a bottle of perfume. He replied that the cost of the bottle was 35 dollars. My next question was: What was the cost of the bottle five years back? The shopkeeper looked at me rather puzzled and clarified, "I beg your pardon. Did you mean what was the price five years back?" I nodded my head. He gestured me to wait, keyed in a few words in his computer and replied, "It was 35 dollars then!" "Was there no inflation in your country?" I asked. To my surprise the shopkeeper replied, "Did you say inflation? Not really!"

Inflation was not known in some of the European countries during the last part of the twentieth century. Today even countries like Austria and Switzerland are going through a difficult time. How should we behave during such a time of high inflation? This is the million-dollar question. In India, inflation has taken a toll on even essential commodities. The government has taken as many steps as possible but has not been able to contain it. In the aftermath of the recession as the economy was sputtering back to life, inflation soared. The investors who kept their hard earned money in the bank already started losing its value. The taxpayer was hit hard. The advantages given in the budget vanished rapidly. Under such dire circumstances many experts proclaimed that the middle-class should stay away from the share market and mutual funds. They should keep their money only in the post office and the bank. Do I subscribe to this view?

During the present volatility, investments should be done through a Systematic Investment Plan only. Invest only if you can hold it for five years. No investment should be done for the short term. I would like to reiterate that the safety of money is the supreme concern. But that does not mean that all people should invest only in debt funds, fixed deposit of banks, and small savings instruments. In an environment of high inflation, money earned from a bank's fixed deposit is a losing proposition. A time will come when the investors may not have enough money to buy the essential commodities of life if they relied only on fixed deposits of banks, post offices and small savings. Only PPF may give them some respite because it used to double its benefits. While depositing money in PPF account, the depositors get matching Income tax deduction from his taxable income, under section 80 C of IT act and while receiving back the money he does not have to pay any tax at all. So while contribution persons get double benefit. Even pensions attract income tax. So what should be done under inflationary pressure?

The middle class should try to avoid non-essential expenses (such as holidays, partying, feasts & festivities) and push back their plans for buying a latest generation motorbike and upgrading their vehicles. These expenses can wait for a while. I am not against enjoying life, but an advocate of planning expenses for the future. It is possible to withstand suffering during our younger days. As we grow old, tensions must be minimal.

What should be done with the saved money? My reply: Invest judiciously.

Where? You should invest, depending on your age, in a bank, PPF, diversified mutual fund, balanced funds, income funds, liquid fund of MF and Arbitrage funds.

Should we take out money from shares, where are we incurring a loss? Taking out money from shares and diversified mutual funds now, would be committing suicide. Let the money remain invested. If you did invest in a weak mutual fund before, then you can switch it to a potentially stronger fund belonging to the SAME Fund House. For example if you invested in Franklyn Prima Fund it can be switched over to Franklyn India Prima Plus. However, this can be done provided you have kept it invested for at least one year. The share market has gone down substantially and it might go down further. But it is bound to bounce back. Stay invested now you will surely be happier person in a couple of years.

Dhirendra Kumar, one of the foremost experts on mutual funds, recently stated that asking the older generation to invest only in bank FDs is really an injustice! This is depriving them from generating the necessary income for a decent life. It is essential that they need to invest 60% in a bank FD, but the rest can be invested in a balanced fund (growth), income fund (monthly expenses) or in a liquid plus fund (for short-term parking). Wealthy senior citizens may be advised to park money in an Arbitrage fund (7% to 9% return) and is the safest of all funds. There are no taxes in these funds if invested for more than a year. Patience is the ladder to cross the volatile sea of share market.

ART AS AN INVESTMENT HAS EMERGED AS THE WINNER

Even in the most tumultuous economic times, gold has been holding its own from time immemorial. After the devastation of World War II, it was gold that helped build up the economy of the west. When Europe found it difficult to move ahead and deflation had set in, it was gold that helped the government and individuals alike in building up their fortunes from scratch.

In the 21st century, it was again gold that showed its value when financial markets crashed all over the world in 2008. In 2009, the Indian markets recovered slightly but in 2010 Europe was again in turmoil when Greece and Spain eroded their net worth as sovereign debt increased and started spiralling out of control. In 2010 also, gold became the darling of governments as well as that of individuals. India bought considerable gold from the IMF during this period.

However, having extolled the virtues of gold, I would like to point out that *paintings and works of art* have emerged as the best investment product even surpassing gold and equity. Among all classes of investment product, equity is considered the king of investment. But the real emperor of the investment product has turned out to be *works of art*.

The paintings of Spanish artists are in great demand in Europe and in America. A Pablo Picasso painting was recently sold for a fortune. A 1932 Pablo Picasso oil painting of his blond mistress Marie-Therese

Walter has fetched a world record price of USD 106.5 million at a
Christie's sale in New York.

Saurashtra, a 7-foot-high, richly-coloured abstract dating from
1983, painted by Indian artist S.H. Raza was expected to sell for
£1.3-1.8 million. But auctioned by Christie's of London on 15th June,
2010, it fetched £2.4 million (Rs. 16.4 crores!) The twelve paintings
of Rabindra Nath Tagore fetched well over Rs. 11 crores. Jogen
Choudhury's painting from Kolkata brought in over Rs. 2.50 core.
These were the same paintings which could not get even Rs. 10
lakhs just ten years back. This kind of high valuation of Indian art
comes after a collection of 152 works by one of the country's most
sought-after modern artists, F.N. Souza fetched £5.4 million with fees,
exceeding a presale upper forecast of £2.3 million, based on hammer
prices, said the representative of auction house.

Speaking exclusively to an Indian newspaper from southern France,
S.H. Raza said, "In all my life, I have worked with a lot of sincerity
and dedication . . . I'm glad to know that there's some result and my
works are being appreciated and understood globally. It's recognition
of the core Indian philosophy that I have tried to depict."

"People have less and less confidence in paper money—you can see
in what's happening with the euro right now—and more confidence
in real things that are lasting, art being one of them," said Berggruen,
who ranked No. 158 on the Forbes list of the 400 richest Americans
in 2009. Berggruen, who is accumulating works for an expansion
of Berlin's Museum, discounted the notion of a bubble forming in
the art market. Two days after the auction, he wondered if maybe he
should have gone further in bidding. Asher Edelman, the founder of
ArtAssure, Ltd., which guarantees prices on portfolios at auction,
said that art has never been in greater demand as an investment and
is sought after by traditional buyers and those in emerging markets.
"You're at the beginning of the up-cycle in art," he said, adding that

international buyers are suddenly playing a much larger role. "It has become an asset class, either subconsciously or consciously, for everybody."

When we look at the Indian art scene, we find similar trends in the art market. M.F. Hussein's painting which was sold in 1980 at Rs. 10 lakh and is in a collector's possession in Assam has been valued at Rs. 3 crore in 2009! It is around 20 core in 2013.The paintings of Sunil Das who lived in Assam for a few years in the nineties would sell for Rs. 10,000/—and now all of his paintings are sold at not less than Rs. 5 lakhs a piece. Ten years back, the paintings of Shyamkanu, Rajbanshi, and Singh (all from Assam) would sell at around Rs. 2000/—Now their paintings and sculptures are sold at a price between Rs. 80 thousand to Rs. 2 lakh each.

We tried to contact a few art dealers in Kolkata and Bombay who confirmed that works of art are recession proof. According to them, works of some selected artists have defied the financial downturn. Now, when the financial market in Europe is in doldrums, works of art are sold at the highest price.

However it should be kept in mind that real works of art are very, very costly and may not be affordable for people belonging to the middle class. But real connoisseurs of art may be able to judge a talented budding artist's work and can buy the product at less cost initially and can sell out for a handsome profit later. We did some research on the valuation of different asset classes. Our work revealed that in twenty years, the best return came from Works of Art, followed by Equity Stock and Mutual Funds, which was followed by Real Estate and Gold. Then what should be our priority?

In my opinion, all middle class young investors should invest in Equity, followed by Bank Fixed Deposits, PPF, and then buy Gold. The investment in Real Estate and Art should be the prerogative of high-net worth persons only. But some art lovers having uncanny eyes to appreciate some brilliant works may buy pieces of art at a reasonable cost now to fetch a high price in the future. We need to keep in mind that art provides the highest return but in reality, Equity is the king in the ten-year tenure.

DO A THOROUGH HOME WORK
MUCH BEFORE RETIRMENT

In India, all employed persons retire after working for at least 34 years on attaining their superannuated age of sixty. There are a few lucky ones who get re-employed for a further period of five years or more. In any case, a day comes when they too would retire from employment and lead a life of peace, prosperity and happiness. This state can be achieved only if one does their proper homework for their post-retirement life. Two persons of the same age, drawing the same salary, and retiring from the same position might live differently, either in happiness or sorrow, depending on their level of preparedness.

Retirement is an inseparable phase of life, and this is probably the most crucial stage of the human life-cycle. People have different kinds of needs in different phases of life; it changes according to age, income, lifestyle, etc. A person generally has five types of needs. They are psychological, safety and security, social, self-esteem, and self-actualization.

Aged people have social and security needs. It does not mean that they had not felt this need before; they had felt it and had satisfied it too. But with the passage of time, they spent a major portion of their earnings either on their children's education or in building a house or on their parents' health. At the end of the day, they forget to keep aside part of their earnings to fulfil their post-retirement needs. This situation is common in most Indian homes.

As we reach old age, we realize that the time and money that we have saved for ourselves may not be sufficient for us to lead a tension-free life after our retirement. In this case, it becomes the duty of the children to look after their parents without making them face any financial problems.

There are some points that you need to know and follow before you reach retirement age. This will help you to lead a comfortable post-retirement life without facing any financial problems. Preparation of a balance sheet, listing savings and investments, insurance needs, children's education, elimination of unwanted expenses, and creation of emergency funds need to be given due precedence as soon as one reaches forty years or so.

It is very important to have a close eye on your Savings and Borrowings. It's a fact of the financial world that the cost of borrowings is always more than earnings from savings. For instance, if you take a personal loan from a bank, they will make you to pay 20-30% annual interest. At the same time if you are investing in the bank, they offer you 7-8% annual interest. So it is always better to clear off the debt if you have cash to spare.

Retirement is the period during which you will not work. So it is necessary to prepare a paper budget or spending plan to update yourself about what your actual living expenses will be once you are not working.

Every person will have two kinds of expenditure—Fixed and Variable—and among them, variable expenditure is more. This means that most of our expenditures can be controlled if we wish to do so. There are some expenses that go away once we are not working: travel to work, eating out, business clothes, etc. Food costs may go down significantly if you eat your daily meals at home. So think well before taking any decision related to expenditure. A wise decision can save you from losing money unnecessarily. Avoid unnecessary expenses and accumulate a portion of this towards your post-retirement expenditure.

Every person should have life insurance cover so that their family will be safe should any misfortune befall them. Term and life insurance are two important types of insurance that can cover the risk of your life. If you are planning to go for a life insurance once you are 50 or more, it will cost you more. So, it is always better to have life insurance cover when you are young. Most of the life insurance companies offer retirement plans. If you are going for a retirement plan, it will help you replace your salary once you are retired. If the right decisions are made when selecting your plan options, your spouse will be able to continue the pension. Term insurance is generally recommended for young people who have debt, dependents, and few assets. However, a life insurance policy may be necessary for estate planning or other purposes.

Expenditure heads should be identified and also given proper attention. Always make sure that you are eliminating unnecessary expenditures, including your children's educational expenditure. The time to fund your children's college education is when they're small and not when they are graduating and you are counting your days of retirement. As we discussed already, list out your expenditures according to priority and avoid all superfluous spending.

Most of the time, people find it difficult to plan their finances. If this is the case, it is best to consult a financial planner for guidance. An efficient planner can get a comprehensive perspective on your whole financial situation and determine if everything is in order and if you are really prepared to face retirement. He can guide you from re-evaluating your portfolio to organizing your priorities.

Most of the studies done on retirement planning has proven that a large percent of people allocate their money to just one single fund. Another major percent of people allocate their money to only two funds. Only a small percentage of people understand the importance of diversifying their funds. Using a diverse mix of funds or multiple ingredients will help you to achieve your investment goals.

Let me explain this point with an example. If your music player is too loud, do you throw it out of the window? Of course not! You simply adjust the volume and get it back to a tolerable listening level. The same applies to your retirement plan. Instead of dropping your plan into the garbage, get an acceptable mix of investments that match your risk tolerance and financial goals. You may have built up a sum of money in the bank, from the sale of a property or by investing wisely. Yet at some point, it will be important for you to actually see the benefit of your hard work. You may then need to consider changing your investment strategy from *growth* to *income*. In order to achieve better returns, you may have been happy taking a risk with some of your money. But can you now afford to lose what has taken you years to build? Investing for income generally means taking a lower risk and seeing the benefit each month or each year in the form of an income payment. Ultimately, it's your money and you should enjoy it!

Before reaching your retirement age you need to make sure that you have set aside sufficient funds for unexpected costs. This buffer will ensure that you avoid using assets allocated for income or growth purposes. As a general rule of thumb, we suggest saving about three to six months worth of expenses for your emergency fund. An emergency could be anything like car repairs, dental work, or travel expenses for a family member's illness or death. Make sure your emergency fund is liquid. Remember to replace emergency funds as soon you use them.

THE MOTHER OF ALL EVIL IS SPECULATION

Gordon Gekko, a seminal character in the film *Wall Street* proudly pronounced: Greed is good. This one liner lit fires in the hearts of many young investors ever since the movie was released in 1987. Many people become millionaires and some lost money. Gordon Gekko is back in the sequel, *Wall Street: Money Never Sleeps,* after serving eighth years in prison for insider trading. His new one liner is: The mother of all evil is speculation.

We are borrowing this famous line to forewarn the young population of the northeast of impending turmoil in the world economy which may lash Europe first and expand into other countries in Asia. We believe forewarning means forearming. Our advice to young people is not to indulge in speculation while planning their investment strategy. They need to be bold but not speculative. They need not quit from investing money unless there is tearing need for cash. Yes, the share market may crash sooner or later. It may go down and push up again immediately! But do not panic at all. If you are already in, do not redeem; rather, stay invested. However no new money should be put in except through SIP.

Despite offering of stimulus package of one trillion Euro, Greece may not be able to survive the economic turmoil. It is now apparent that Portugal, Spain and Italy my also get effected badly. The fiscal condition of England is not too good. So, the new Prime Minister of Great Britain has not only proposed salary cuts for Ministers but is also planning to reduce jobs in governmental are panicking. Experts such as former Federal Reserve chairman Paul Volcker and Deutsche Bank chief executive Josef Ackermann doubt the strength of financial markets in Europe. Let us not behave like an Ostrich, hiding our head in the sand.

"Greece may not be able to repay its debt in full," Ackermann was quoted by Bloomberg News. Volcker has said that the Euro may break up, and Chinese Premier Wen Jiabo said the foundations for a worldwide recovery are not "solid" as the sovereign debt crisis deepens. What could be done by Indian investors?

Investors flocked to gold, the traditional store of value, pushing it up to a new record of Rs. 18,339 for 10 gm. The coincidence of the auspicious Akshaya Tritiya during last weekend, perhaps added to its strength. Emerging market equity funds had a second straight week of redemptions, according to EPFR data. China equity funds posted their second straight week of outflows and Latin America equity funds saw outflows rise to the highest in 85 weeks. Despite all these turmoil, India is expected to survive better than most other countries. It is not because Indian economy is very vibrant. This may trigger a sudden impact on the fragile economy of Europe. The monetary system may collapse. What would be the condition of the Euro and the Pound Sterling? Both the currencies are going to take a beating. Already, the Euro has come down considerably. It is expected to go down further unless all the countries of Europe start austerity measures.

"The European Economic and Monetary Union (EMU) and the euro are about to celebrate their 10th anniversary. The euro was introduced without serious problems and has since done well" said Martin Feldstein, George F. Baker Professor of Economics at Harvard University. But now he feels that the current economic crisis may provide a severe test of the Euro's ability to survive in more troubled times. While the crisis could strengthen the institutions provided by the EMU, it could also create multiple risks, of which member countries need to be aware if they want to avoid them.

"The Stability and Growth Pact, which limits euro-zone members' fiscal deficits, is another reason why a country might want to leave the EMU. In a serious downturn, a country may wish to pursue a traditional Keynesian policy through large-scale, deficit-financed fiscal stimulus," the Harvard professor of Economics stated. This may boomerang on the economy of member countries.

Many investors are also asking how the Indian economy would be affected. Initially FII may withdraw money from the Indian share market to support its own currencies. The export-based industry of India might take a beating. IT majors who were aggressively pursuing business in Europe may suffer too. In the short term, the share market might go down but it will stabilise in the longer term.

How should the investors of northeast behave to survive the turmoil? According to our considered opinion, the investors of the northeast should hold their money with them. They should keep it in a bank or in the liquid sector of a mutual fund. Money can even be parked in a government-guaranteed bond or Gilt fund. In these instruments, the investor may get 4% to 12% return over the year. They can start investing once the market stabilises at the lower end of the index. If Europe takes a spin, our Sensex and Nifty may plummet. At that time, senior citizens may stop investing in mutual funds, the share market, or in equities. They can invest in a debt-based fund, especially in government-guaranteed debt funds where returns would improve in such a situation.

Global investors, who bought Indian shares worth $6 billion this year due to cheap funds in their home nations and prospects for growth here, are showing signs of taking some gains off the table following more than doubling of stock values. Foreign funds sold Rs 381.42 crore of shares during last week. It is because Indian mass can survive with bare minimum needs for a prolonged time.The 70% of the population in India are below poverty level. This population can remain unaffected even when the Sensex sinks below 12000 points. In 2008, when the growth of the Indian economy was under a cloud, no one died of hunger and no revolution broke out like other Asian countries. It is because, traditionally, Indians know how to survive the worst situations. This is because of the fact that 80% of the population is dependent on agriculture. The failure of monsoon creates a much bigger turmoil rather than a crash of the share market. The biggest support system is the internal market of the country. The needs of the teeming millions are very meagre. People get satisfied if one and half meals are available. A market crash is inconsequential for them.

So, how should the Indian middle class behave if recession strikes us again? Our suggestion is that no senior citizen should enter the share market now. The young generation should hold money and get ready to invest when the market stabilizes at the lower end of the spectrum. Buying of gold can be taken up on a dip in prices. All investments now should be made in debt instruments and investment in equity should start as the market goes down considerably. No investment should be made following the example of your neighbours and friends who boast of making money from equity investments in the past. Please do not listen to the advice of your neighbourhood brokers who have shown you the Golden Goose of equity investment. Patience and a mature handling of wealth will help you survive the catastrophe . . . if it strikes.

THE SHARE MARKET WILL BOOM SOON
BUT NEEDS CAUTIOUS STEPS NOW

After a long time, most middle class investors are smiling again. The share market Sensex touched the 19,000 mark again after January 2008. Is it the beginning of a bull market after a breather? Floods of telephone calls have started pouring in from our readers. "What should I do? I have doubled the amount. Should I redeem it or keep the money invested?" My reply to young investors was to stay invested if they do not want the money for the next four years. There will be a correction but again the market will go up. For seniors, whose appetite for risk is low, they need to switch money to liquid funds and park the money for a while to invest when market corrects after sometime.

Another gentleman asked, "Can I redeem the money and keep it in debt fund for a while and reinvest when market goes down?" It is a good idea no doubt, but if the money is kept invested in a debt fund you cannot shift to another fund within one year without paying an exit load. So if you redeem it now keep it in your savings account or in a liquid fund so that you can reinvest it the moment the market goes down. The pessimism in the investment community is understandable as markets are nowhere near being called cheap. The price to earning (P/E) ratios are well over 22-23 and the continued fund flow has made sure that the selling pressures from domestic fund houses hasn't been a deterrent for the bulls. The new action on the repo rate by RBI will also hit the mutual fund market, debt funds, and MIPs. That in turn would affect senior citizens.

According to mutual fund industry sources, the selling pressures from domestic institutions have been on account of redemption pressures from individual investors. In fact, individual investor behaviour has been that of caution in the last two years. Having been caught on the wrong foot in 2008, the small investor is in no mood to think long-term. As a result, during every uptrend, many have been quick to sell and cash in for profits or cut down losses—especially, those who built their portfolios in 2007-08. In the process, they failed to ride on the good market mood of the last few years.

The Bombay Stock Exchange (BSE) Sensex and the National Stock Exchange Nifty crossed a landmark each during the early session of trading on Monday. While the Sensex breached the 18,500 level, the Nifty crossed 5,400 marks on strong industrial output numbers from Asian and the US economies. But keep in mind that the P/E ratio is not as high as it was during January 2008. At that time the P/E ratio was 28. So the market may go up further. It is sure to correct at some time when liquidity comes down.

Banking stocks showed the sharpest jump in the early session as the Sensex and Nifty rose by close to 3% at 11 AM. The small—and mid-cap stocks, however, lagged both the Nifty and the Sensex. This rally seems more liquidity driven and is not fundamental driven alone. The participation from retail investors of the country is minimal. They remained hesitant even now to invest. Of course, there is a strong possibility of a deep correction from 10% to 20% at any time. So our advice to the hesitant lot is to keep away from equity mutual funds.

Perhaps, they can invest in long-term MIPs where return is around 9 to 12% from time to time. There are three good funds in this segment according to value research—Birla Sunlife MIP, Reliance MIP, and HDFC MIP. These funds have got 5 to 25% equity and the balance is in debt. My personal favourites are HDFC and Reliance MIP for retired persons. HDFC MIP has paid in 71 times dividend in 77 months. The average annual dividends for the last six years is around 11%, which is much more than a bank FD, company FD, and SCSS but with little risk. This is the time to invest in a long-term corporate bond fund, FMPs and short and medium term debt funds.

My sincere advice to our readers is not to invest any more once the Sensex reaches 20,000 points or a little lower. That would be time to redeem the investment if they have earned a good profit and have completed at least one year or more. Keep your money handy to invest when the market goes down. There is a strong possibility of correction. Invest all the money when correction sets in. People who have done STP or SIP do not have to worry at all. They should keep on investing even while the market goes down. The long-term investors have nothing to worry about. They will surely make money.

We need to understand that share market is a risky field and correction is inevitable. Warren Buffet makes money because the share market is a volatile field and he enters the market when others fly away. He invests in companies whose functioning he understands well. It is impossible for the rest of us to understand such nuances. So, it is wise to depend on your personal financial advisors for advice. Investors at least need to study *Money* magazine and the business pages of newspapers and form their own opinion.

On the flip side, the key concern area of inflation is also likely to moderate as we go forward, resulting in most of the monetary tightening measures being front ended. This, along with the strong earnings growth momentum, wherein the Sensex earnings are expected to grow, at an 18 percent CAGR over FY2010-12. Indian equities will continue to grow and gradually move upwards in the long run. In the short—and mid-term there could be a correction.

It is necessary for senior citizens to understand that they need not invest all their money in an equity related instrument. They can invest only 20-30% money in equity. The balance money could be kept invested in PPF, SCSS and Banks FD and a long term debt fund. While investing in equity, they should invest mostly in balanced fund like HDFC Prudence or Reliance Balanced Fund. They can invest also in MIP of HDFC and Reliance or in Birla.

Younger readers can take risk and can invest a larger amount in equity. But they too need not put all the eggs in one basket. Good diversified funds are IDFC Premier Equity, HDFC Equity and Top 200 besides Reliance Growth and Birla Dividend Yield. Invest through a Systematic Investment Plan (SIP).

Asian equity markets also rose in September on the back of strong economic data in China and the United States. The news on agreement among global banking regulators to implement stricter Basel III norms also stoked positive sentiments in the market.

Japan's benchmark Nikkei average rose 1.4 per cent, while the MSCI index of Asian shares outside Japan was up 1.6 per cent as strong economic numbers boosted investors' confidence. India's growth story is taking shape and this is the time our readers should take advantage of the share market of the country. The bottom line is that patience is the most necessary virtue if investors want to make money. Be a long-term player. Redeem your funds whenever you make more than a 30% return. Keep it aside for some time to reinvest when the market goes down. Rakesh Jhunjunwala said that he enjoys when the market goes down because only then can he make money in the future.

SOME OFT-ASKED QUESTIONS BY YOUNG INVESTORS OF INDIA

All investors are inquisitive. They have lots of questions in their minds. Some ask openly, but a few do not ask directly and wait for someone to ask the questions on their behalf. Here are some questions that we have often encountered. Answers to which follow. But the more knowledgeable can answer them better. We welcome well thought out answers as measure of service to new young investors. Here we go.

Q: Is investment in diversified mutual fund better than ULIP?

A: ULIP and Diversified Mutual Funds belong to two different classes of asset base. ULIP is not an investment product. It is an insurance product. So it is a costly product compared to any mutual fund. ULIP is very good if taken for longer period say for ten to fifteen years. It is ideal for saving money for children's education or marriage. In short term, it does not give an adequate return. So if ULIP is redeemed within three to four years there is every possibility of incurring a loss. Diversified Mutual Fund is an investment product and is less costly. Nowadays, there is no entry load. There are exit loads if redeemed before one year. The administration charges are lower at around 2 to 2.5% only. So if somebody wants to invest for four to five years only, it should be in Diversified Equity Funds. ULIP also provides security which mutual fund does not give. ULIP is good for long term planning.

Q: Should we take insurance cover first or invest in mutual fund first?

A: This issue would depend on the requirement of the person concerned. If the person has to bear the responsibilities of a family, s/he surely needs to take insurance. But in case the person does not have family obligations, s/he can opt for investment first. Insurance is not an investment. It provides security and safety to the family. This is a very important social requirement for a person who is the *karta*. Without family obligations, a person is free to start with the investment option. But as soon as s/he gets married and has children, s/he needs to protect the family with the insurance option.

Q: For any investment, who should we depend on? Should we depend on agents, brokers or should we study ourselves?

A: The best thing to do is to study on your own. The money belongs to you. You are the best person to protect your own money. Knowledge is power. So you need to acquire knowledge. If you cannot study due to time constraints or lack of opportunity, you should depend on wise and educated professional advisers. All regular brokers and agents may not be as reliable as you expect. So you need to select your own reliable professional advisors. Some good banks have their own investment department. You can depend on them. You can also speak with a qualified, knowledgeable chartered accountant or economist. But the best of all is to study yourself before you invest.

Q: How much should one invest?

A: There is no definite answer to this question. After meeting your family obligations, whatever amount is available can be invested after setting aside a portion of it for emergency purposes. Many people save around 30% of their annual earnings.

Q: Where should we invest—shares, mutual fund or in gold?

A: Everyone should begin investing regularly in a bank, followed by PPF and small savings schemes. Slowly investments should be made in diversified mutual funds and later in shares. No one should begin investing in the share market. It would be dangerous.

Q: How long should one plan to invest in mutual funds or in shares?

A: No one should invest in equity for the short term. It would be suicidal to invest for one year or two years. Any investment in equity should be made if the person concerned can keep the money invested for at least four to five years.

QUESTION: Which are the best funds where investment can be made now?

ANSWER: Your personal financial advisers will help you in this regard. You should regularly study the personal finance page in the *Business Standard, Economic Times, The Assam Tribune* and *The Hindu*. These newspapers carry articles on investment that usually appear every Monday. You can also read *Money* magazine and watch CNBC TV. You can also visit www.valueresearch.com and moneycontrol.com and select five star and four star funds.

To be successful investors the motto of the investor should be Hope for the best in the long term (Ten Years) and prepare yourself for the worst in the short term.
